At Sylvan, we believe reading is one of life's most important, most personal, most meaningful skills, and we're so glad you've taken this step to build a strong vocabulary with us. Vocabulary knowledge has a direct effect on reading comprehension, and reading comprehension is the foundation of success in all aspects of fourth-grade academics and beyond. As a successful reader, you hold infinite possibilities in your hands, enabling you to learn about anything and everything. That's because the more you read, the more you learn. And the more you learn, the more connections you can make to the world around you.

At Sylvan, successful vocabulary instruction encompasses numerous vocabulary acquisition processes with research-based, developmentally appropriate, and highly motivating, entertaining, and thought-provoking lessons. The learning process relies on high standards and meaningful parental involvement. With success, students feel increasing confidence. With increasing confidence, students build even more success. It's a perfect cycle. That's why our Sylvan workbooks aren't like the others. We're laying out the roadmap for learning. The rest is in your hands.

Parents, you have a special role. While your child is working, stay within earshot. If he needs help or gets stuck, you can be there to get him on the right track. And you're always there with supportive encouragement and plenty of celebratory congratulations.

One of the best ways to study vocabulary is to check one's own work. Often the answer is just a dictionary away, so that's always a good place to start. Each section of the workbook also includes a Check It! strip. As your child completes the activities, he can check his answers with Check It! If he sees any errors, he can fix them himself.

At Sylvan, our goal is fluent and strategic readers who have the skills to tackle anything they want to read. We love learning. We want all children to love it as well.

Included with your purchase is a coupon for a discount on our in-center service. As your child continues on his academic journey, your local Sylvan Learning Center can partner with your family in ensuring your child remains a confident, successful, and independent learner.

The Sylvan Team

4th-Grade Vocabulary Success

Published in the United States by Random House, Inc.,New York, and in Canada by Random House of Canada Limited, Toronto.

www.tutoring.sylvanlearning.com

Created by Smarterville Productions LLC
Cover and Interior Photos: Jonathan Pozniak
Cover and Interior Illustrations: Duendes del Sur

First Edition

ISBN: 978-0-375-43005-3

Library of Congress Cataloging-in-Publication Data available upon request.

This book is available at special discounts for bulk purchases for sales promotions or premiums. For more information, write to Special Markets/Premium Sales, 1745 Broadway, MD 6-2, New York, New York 10019 or e-mail specialmarkets@randomhouse.com.

PRINTED IN CHINA

10 9 8 7 6 5 4 3 2 1

Contents

Checking your answers is part of the learning.

Each section of the workbook begins with an easy-to-use Check It! strip.

1. Before beginning the activities, cut out the Check It! strip.

2. As you complete the activities on each page, check your answers.

3. If you find an error, you can correct it yourself.

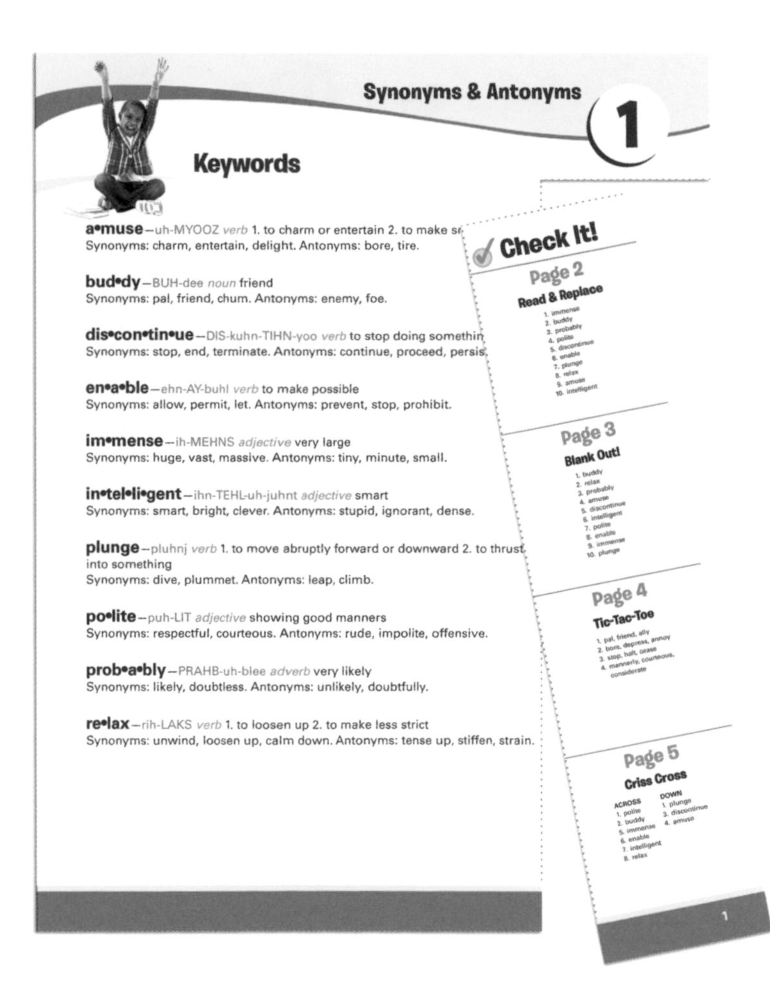

Synonyms & Antonyms

1

Keywords

a•muse—uh-MYOOZ *verb* 1. to charm or entertain 2. to make sr
Synonyms: charm, entertain, delight. Antonyms: bore, tire.

bud•dy—BUH-dee *noun* friend
Synonyms: pal, friend, chum. Antonyms: enemy, foe.

dis•con•tin•ue—DIS-kuhn-TIHN-yoo *verb* to stop doing somethin
Synonyms: stop, end, terminate. Antonyms: continue, proceed, persis

en•a•ble—ehn-AY-buhl *verb* to make possible
Synonyms: allow, permit, let. Antonyms: prevent, stop, prohibit.

im•mense—ih-MEHNS *adjective* very large
Synonyms: huge, vast, massive. Antonyms: tiny, minute, small.

in•tel•li•gent—ihn-TEHL-uh-juhnt *adjective* smart
Synonyms: smart, bright, clever. Antonyms: stupid, ignorant, dense.

plunge—pluhnj *verb* 1. to move abruptly forward or downward 2. to thrust into something
Synonyms: dive, plummet. Antonyms: leap, climb.

po•lite—puh-LIT *adjective* showing good manners
Synonyms: respectful, courteous. Antonyms: rude, impolite, offensive.

prob•a•bly—PRAHB-uh-blee *adverb* very likely
Synonyms: likely, doubtless. Antonyms: unlikely, doubtfully.

re•lax—rih-LAKS *verb* 1. to loosen up 2. to make less strict
Synonyms: unwind, loosen up, calm down. Antonyms: tense up, stiffen, strain.

Check It!

Page 2
Read & Replace
1. immense
2. buddy
3. probably
4. polite
5. discontinue
6. enable
7. plunge
8. relax
9. amuse
10. intelligent

Page 3
Blank Out!
1. buddy
2. relax
3. probably
4. amuse
5. discontinue
6. intelligent
7. polite
8. enable
9. immense
10. plunge

Page 4
Tic-Tac-Toe
1. pal, friend, ally
2. bore, depress, annoy
3. stop, halt, cease
4. mannerly, courteous, considerate

Page 5
Criss Cross

ACROSS
1. polite
2. buddy
5. immense
6. enable
7. intelligent
8. relax

DOWN
1. plunge
3. discontinue
4. amuse

1

Keywords

a•muse—uh-MYOOZ *verb* 1. to charm or entertain 2. to make smile or laugh
Synonyms: charm, entertain, delight. Antonyms: bore, tire.

bud•dy—BUH-dee *noun* friend
Synonyms: pal, friend, chum. Antonyms: enemy, foe.

dis•con•tin•ue—DIS-kuhn-TIHN-yoo *verb* to stop doing something
Synonyms: stop, end, terminate. Antonyms: continue, proceed, persist.

en•a•ble—ehn-AY-buhl *verb* to make possible
Synonyms: allow, permit, let. Antonyms: prevent, stop, prohibit.

im•mense—ih-MEHNS *adjective* very large
Synonyms: huge, vast, massive. Antonyms: tiny, minute, small.

in•tel•li•gent—ihn-TEHL-uh-juhnt *adjective* smart
Synonyms: smart, bright, clever. Antonyms: stupid, ignorant, dense.

plunge—pluhnj *verb* 1. to move abruptly forward or downward 2. to thrust into something
Synonyms: dive, plummet. Antonyms: leap, climb.

po•lite—puh-LIT *adjective* showing good manners
Synonyms: respectful, courteous. Antonyms: rude, impolite, offensive.

prob•a•bly—PRAHB-uh-blee *adverb* very likely
Synonyms: likely, doubtless. Antonyms: unlikely, doubtfully.

re•lax—rih-LAKS *verb* 1. to loosen up 2. to make less strict
Synonyms: unwind, loosen up, calm down. Antonyms: tense up, stiffen, strain.

Check It!

Page 2

Read & Replace

1. immense
2. buddy
3. probably
4. polite
5. discontinue
6. enable
7. plunge
8. relax
9. amuse
10. intelligent

Page 3

Blank Out!

1. buddy
2. relax
3. probably
4. amuse
5. discontinue
6. intelligent
7. polite
8. enable
9. immense
10. plunge

Page 4

Tic-Tac-Toe

1. pal, friend, ally
2. bore, depress, annoy
3. stop, halt, cease
4. mannerly, courteous, considerate

Page 5

Criss Cross

ACROSS
1. polite
2. buddy
5. immense
6. enable
7. intelligent
8. relax

DOWN
1. plunge
3. discontinue
4. amuse

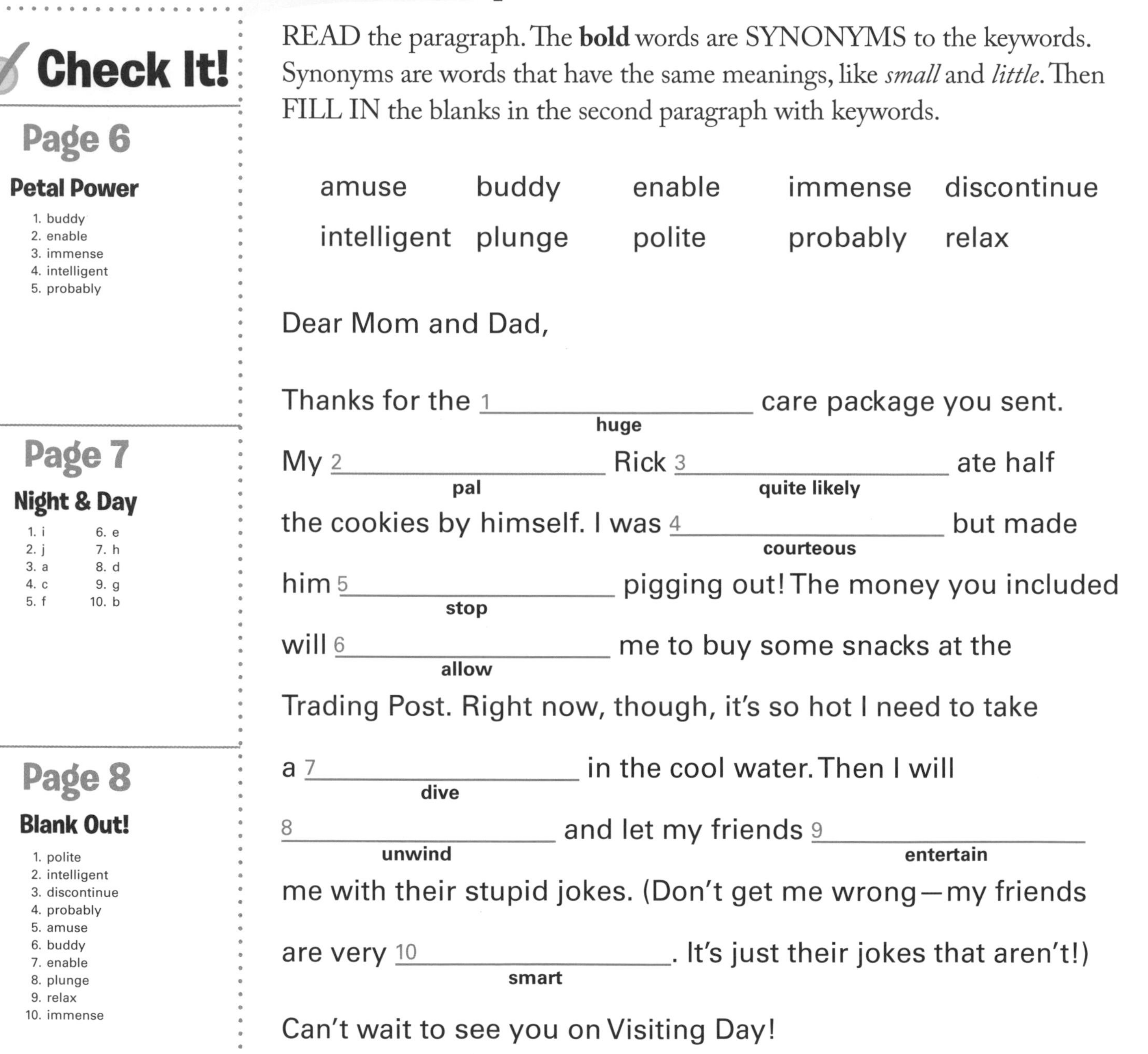

Read & Replace

READ the paragraph. The **bold** words are SYNONYMS to the keywords. Synonyms are words that have the same meanings, like *small* and *little*. Then FILL IN the blanks in the second paragraph with keywords.

amuse	buddy	enable	immense	discontinue
intelligent	plunge	polite	probably	relax

Dear Mom and Dad,

Thanks for the 1 ______________ (**huge**) care package you sent. My 2 ______________ (**pal**) Rick 3 ______________ (**quite likely**) ate half the cookies by himself. I was 4 ______________ (**courteous**) but made him 5 ______________ (**stop**) pigging out! The money you included will 6 ______________ (**allow**) me to buy some snacks at the Trading Post. Right now, though, it's so hot I need to take a 7 ______________ (**dive**) in the cool water. Then I will 8 ______________ (**unwind**) and let my friends 9 ______________ (**entertain**) me with their stupid jokes. (Don't get me wrong—my friends are very 10 ______________ (**smart**). It's just their jokes that aren't!)

Can't wait to see you on Visiting Day!

Max

Check It!

Page 6

Petal Power

1. buddy
2. enable
3. immense
4. intelligent
5. probably

Page 7

Night & Day

1. i	6. e
2. j	7. h
3. a	8. d
4. c	9. g
5. f	10. b

Page 8

Blank Out!

1. polite
2. intelligent
3. discontinue
4. probably
5. amuse
6. buddy
7. enable
8. plunge
9. relax
10. immense

Blank Out!

FILL IN the blanks with keywords. Each sentence contains an ANTONYM of a keyword in **bold**. Antonyms are words that have opposite meanings, like *fast* and *slow*.

amuse	buddy	enable	immense	discontinue
intelligent	plunge	polite	probably	relax

1. At first she was my **enemy**, but now she's my buddy.
2. If studying made you **tense**, you can relax by shooting some hoops.
3. It seemed **unlikely** that she would win, but she will probably be the class president.
4. Though the first act might **bore** you, the second one will definitely amuse you.
5. Hit "OK" to **keep going** or "Cancel" to discontinue.
6. Many people think birds are **stupid**, but they are actually very intelligent.
7. Even though my brother is **rude** to me, I try to be polite to him.
8. Playing basketball might **prevent** you from getting better, but staying home will enable you to get well.
9. We walked through a **little** park and then got to an immense field.
10. The rollercoaster **climbed** to the top before it began to plunge downward.

Tic-Tac-Toe

PLAY Tic-tac-toe with synonyms and antonyms. CIRCLE any word that is a synonym to the blue word. PUT an X through any antonyms. When you find three synonyms or antonyms in a row, you are a winner! The line can go up and down, across, or diagonally.

HINT: If you find a word you don't know, check a dictionary or thesaurus.

Example:

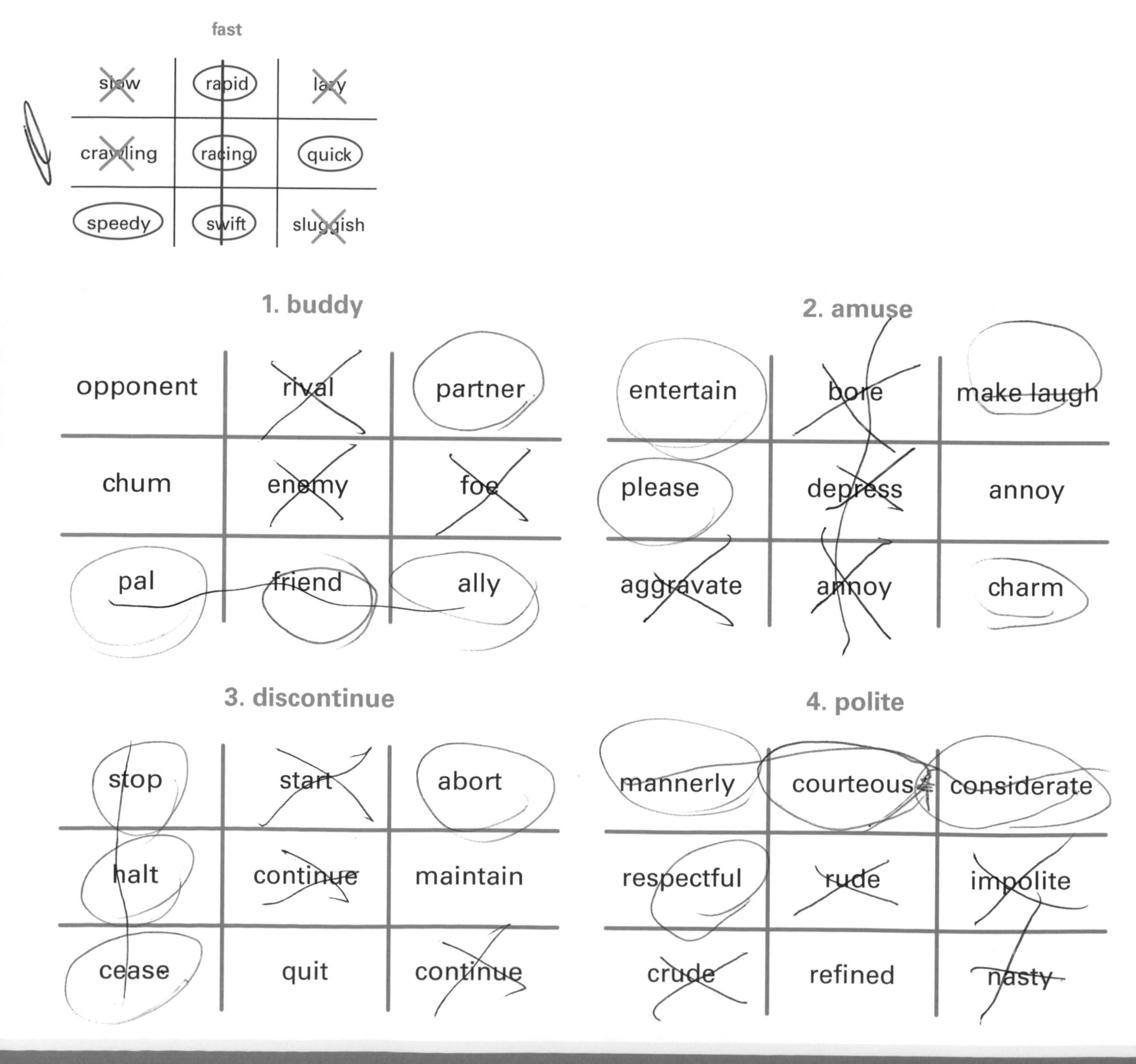

fast

slow	rapid	lazy
crawling	racing	quick
speedy	swift	sluggish

1. buddy

opponent	rival	partner
chum	enemy	foe
pal	friend	ally

2. amuse

entertain	bore	make laugh
please	depress	annoy
aggravate	annoy	charm

3. discontinue

stop	start	abort
halt	continue	maintain
cease	quit	continue

4. polite

mannerly	courteous	considerate
respectful	rude	impolite
crude	refined	nasty

Criss Cross

FILL IN the grid by answering the clues with keywords. The clues are all synonyms of the keywords.

ACROSS

1. Say thank you to be _____.
2. To be safe, stick with your ____ on the field trip.
5. The size of an elephant
6. Help something happen
7. Smart
8. Let loose

DOWN

1. When you don't hesitate to get in the pool
3 Cease
4. Delight

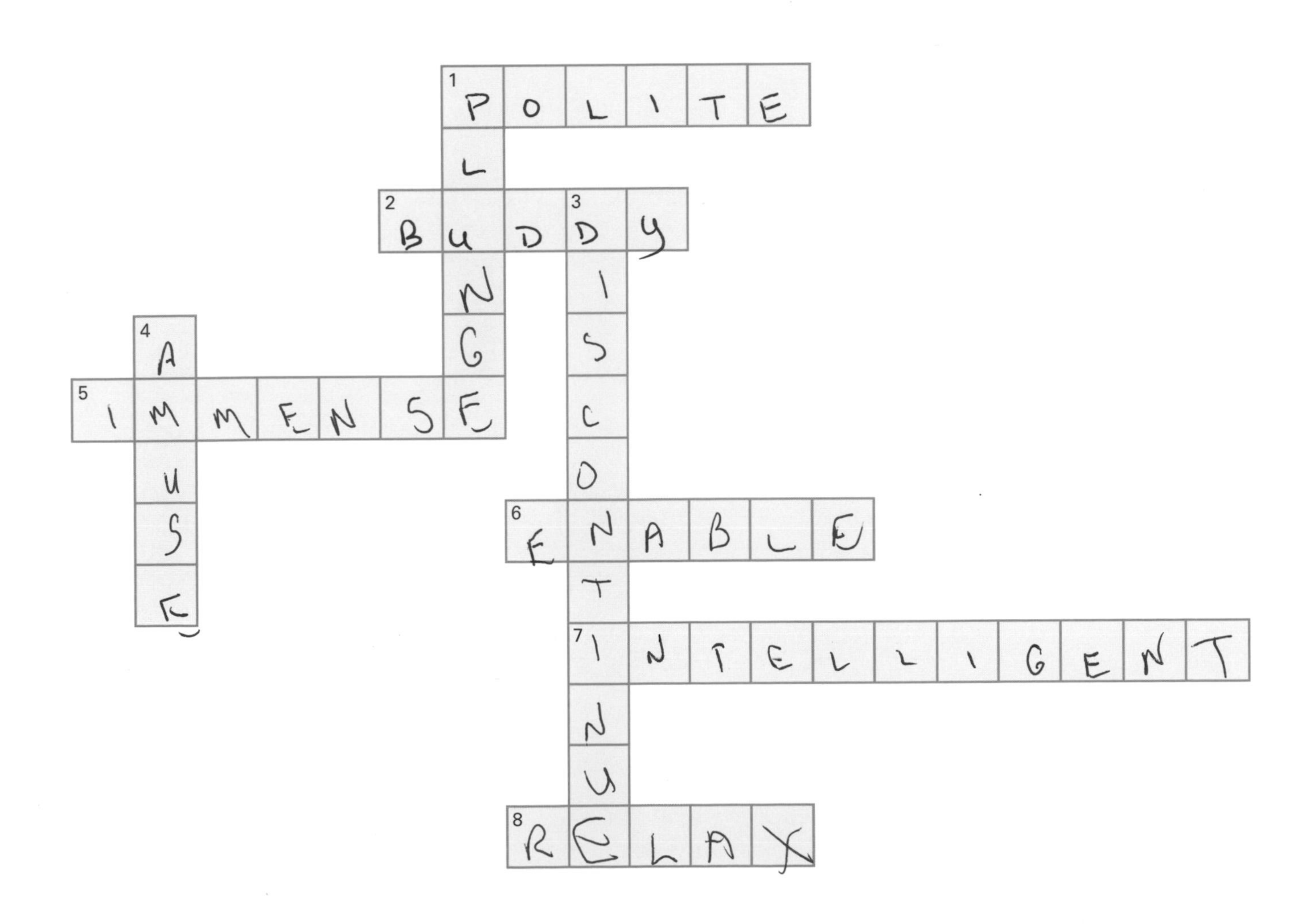

Petal Power

The petals around the flowers are ANTONYMS to the word in the center. Antonyms are words that have opposite meanings, like *tiny* and *huge*. READ the words around each flower. Then WRITE the keyword that's their antonym in the center.

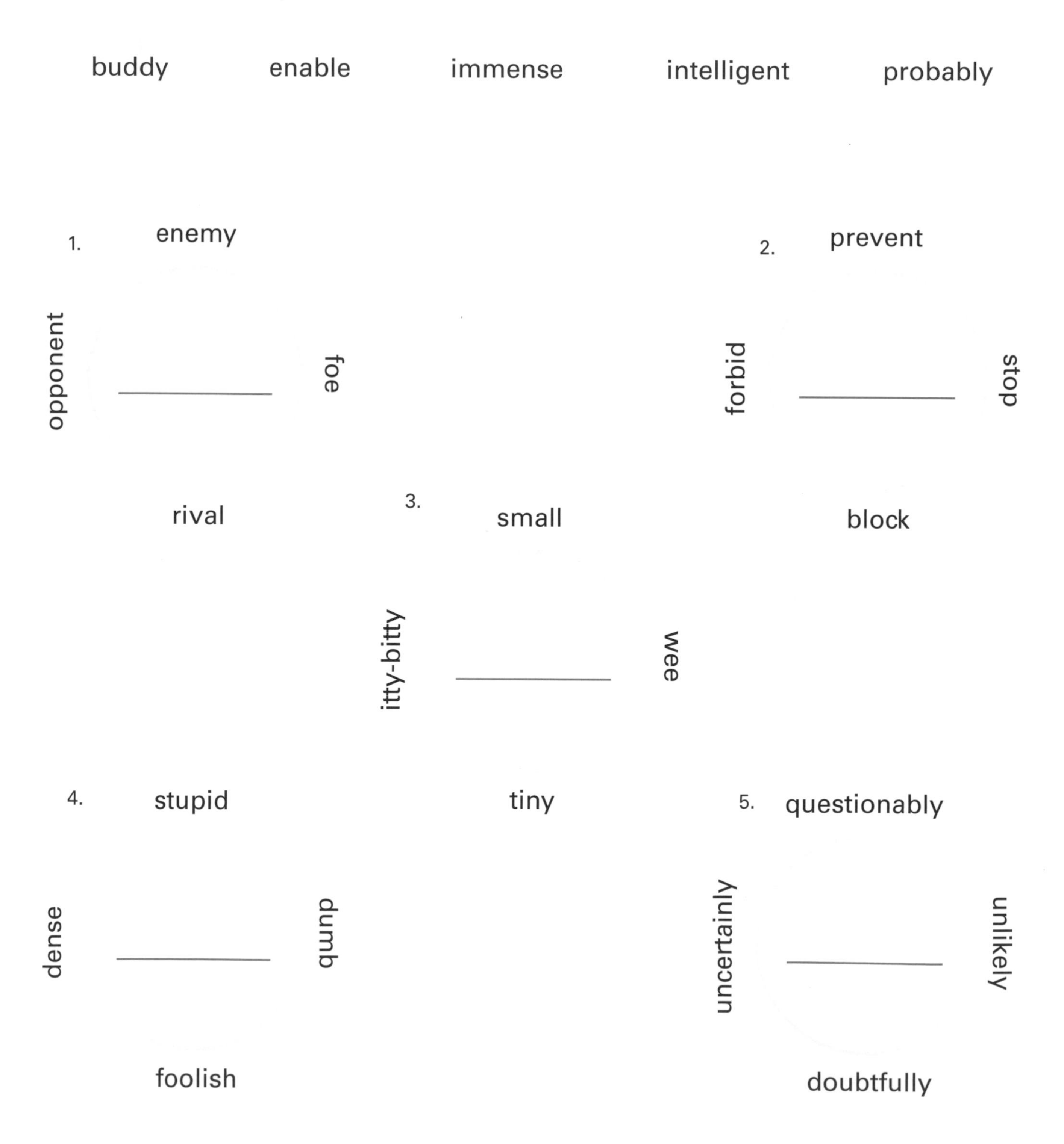

Night & Day

MATCH each word in the moon column to its antonym in the sun column.

1. plunge	a. prevent
2. probably	b. enemy
3. enable	c. rude
4. polite	d. keep going
5. intelligent	e. small
6. immense	f. stupid
7. relax	g. bore
8. discontinue	h. tense up
9. amuse	i. climb
10. buddy	j. unlikely

Blank Out!

FILL in the blanks with keywords.

1. Saying "please" and "thank you" is being ________________.
2. Someone who gets straight A's is ________________.
3. When you no longer want a magazine subscription, you ________________ it.
4. I brought my umbrella because the weather report said that it would ________________ rain.
5. Jokes and riddles ________________ us.
6. I like to hang out with my ________________.
7. When you help someone get something done, you ________________ them.
8. If it's hot tomorrow, let's ________________ into a cool pool.
9. After raking leaves for hours, I like to ________________.
10. Something humongous is ________________.

Check It!

Cut out the Check It! section on page 1, and see if you got the answers right.

Keywords

a•loud—uh-LOWD *adverb* 1. using the voice 2. not silently

al•lowed—uh-LOWD *verb (past tense)* permitted

creak—kreek *verb* to make a squeaking sound

creek—kreek *noun* a small stream

hour—owr *noun* 1. a unit of time equaling 60 minutes 2. the time of day

our—owr *pronoun* belonging to us

prin•ci•pal—PRIHN-suh-puhl *noun* 1. the head of a school 2. the main leader of an activitiy or group

prin•ci•ple—PRIHN-suh-puhl *noun* a belief or value that helps guide behavior

sighs—siz *verb* breathes out audibly *noun* the sounds of sighing

size—siz *noun* 1. how big something is 2. the physical dimensions of an object

Check It!

Page 10

Blank Out!

1. principal
2. our
3. creek
4. hour
5. aloud
6. allowed
7. size
8. creak
9. principle
10. sighs

Page 11

Homophone Hopscotch

1. hour
2. principal
3. sighs
4. our
5. allowed
6. creek
7. principle
8. size
9. aloud
10. creak

Page 12

It's Puzzling!

1. aloud, D. allowed
2. creak, B. creek
3. principal, E. principle
4. size, A. sighs
5. our, C. hour

Page 13

Criss Cross

ACROSS	DOWN
2. our	1. principal
3. size	3. sighs
5. hour	4. creak
7. allowed	6. creek

Blank Out!

HOMOPHONES are words that sound the same but have different meanings. *Too*, *two*, and *to* are homophones. READ the story. Then FILL IN the blanks with keywords.

aloud	allowed	creak	creek	hour
our	principal	principle	sighs	size

We had an assembly at school today. The 1 ________________ told us that a special activity was going to take place that afternoon. As part of a nature program, 2 ________________ entire grade was going to walk to a nearby 3 ________________. We would spend an 4 ________________ studying the land, water, and wildlife. She said that no talking 5 ________________ would be 6 ________________. I knew that would be hard for my buddy, Benny.

The creek was small, but I could not believe the 7 ________________ of the frogs and minnows. Right off, Benny fell in! His wet shoes started to 8 ________________. That scared all the frogs away! Then he began making *ribbit!* noises, hopping like a frog and chasing after them. Thanks to Benny, we all got a lesson on the 9 ________________ of not disturbing nature. And the teacher learned not to go with Benny on any more nature walks! All too soon, the hour was up. There were many 10 ________________ from the teacher as we headed back inside.

Check It!

Page 14

Blank Out!

1. hour
2. size
3. allowed
4. creak
5. sighs
6. principle
7. aloud
8. our
9. principal
10. creek

Page 15

Double Trouble

1. principal
2. allowed
3. sighs
4. hour
5. principle
6. our
7. aloud
8. creak
9. size
10. creek

Page 16

Blank Out!

1. size
2. principle
3. our
4. allowed
5. aloud
6. sighs
7. creek
8. principal
9. creak
10. hour

Homophone Hopscotch

LOOK AT the definitions. FIND the matching keyword, and put it in the box with the same number.

aloud	allowed	creak	creek	hour
our	principal	principle	sighs	size

1. 60 minutes
2. head of school
3. lets out a loud breath
4. belonging to us
5. permitted
6. small stream
7. strong belief
8. how big something is
9. not silently
10. squeaking sound

10. ____________

8. ____________ 9. ____________

7. ____________

5. ____________ 6. ____________

4. ____________

2. ____________ 3. ____________

1. ____________

Bonus

SHADE in the boxes with colored pencils. Use the same color for each pair of homophones.

It's Puzzling!

FILL IN a keyword to solve each clue. MATCH each puzzle piece to its homophone partner.

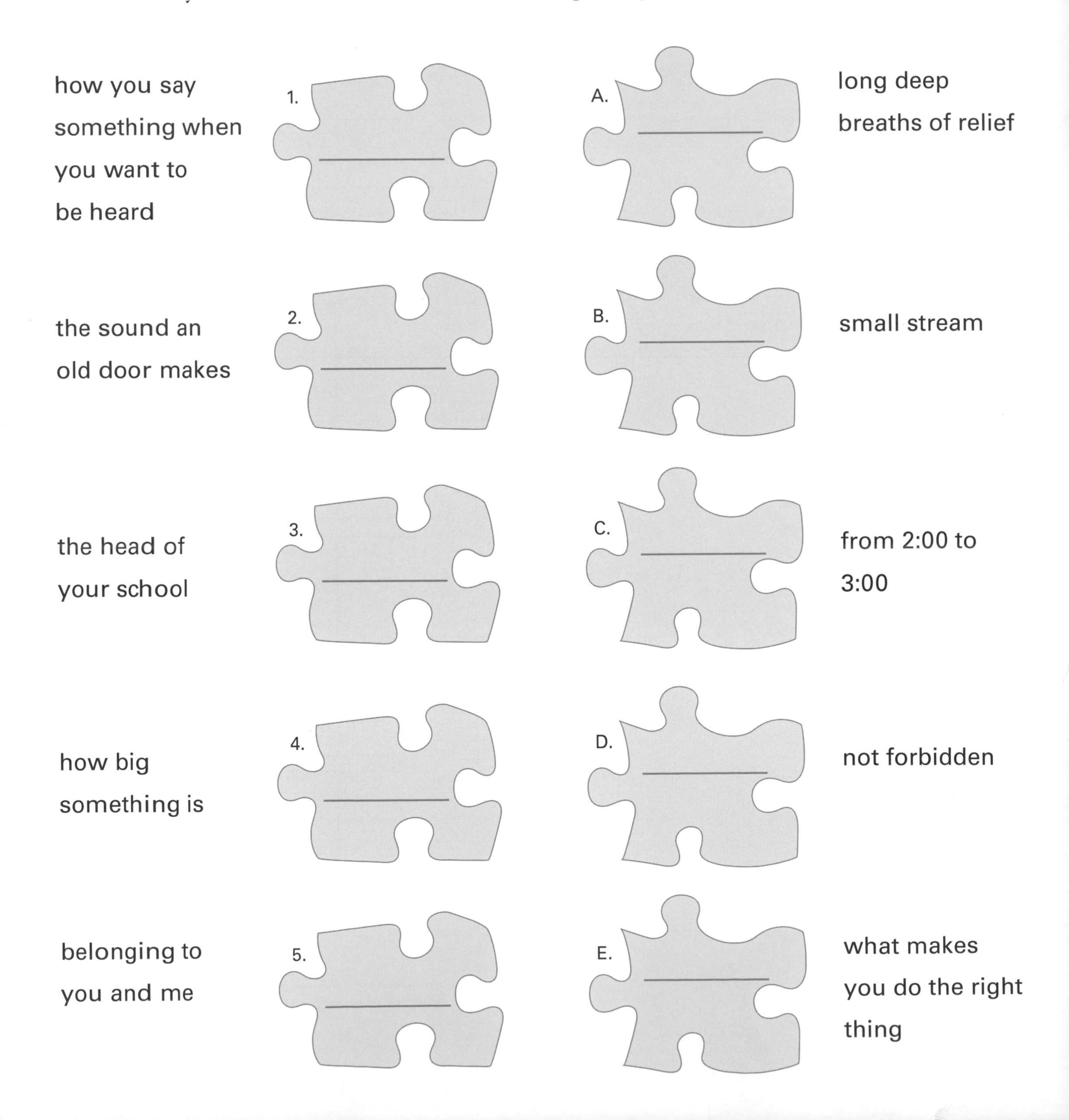

Criss Cross

FILL IN the grid by answering the clues with keywords.

ACROSS

2. We share a book, so it's ___ book.
3. Physical dimensions
5. Unit of time
7. You're not ___ to go there.

DOWN

1. Vice principal's boss
3. Sounds of relief or boredom
4. Old floorboards sometimes do this
6. A place where you might catch small fish

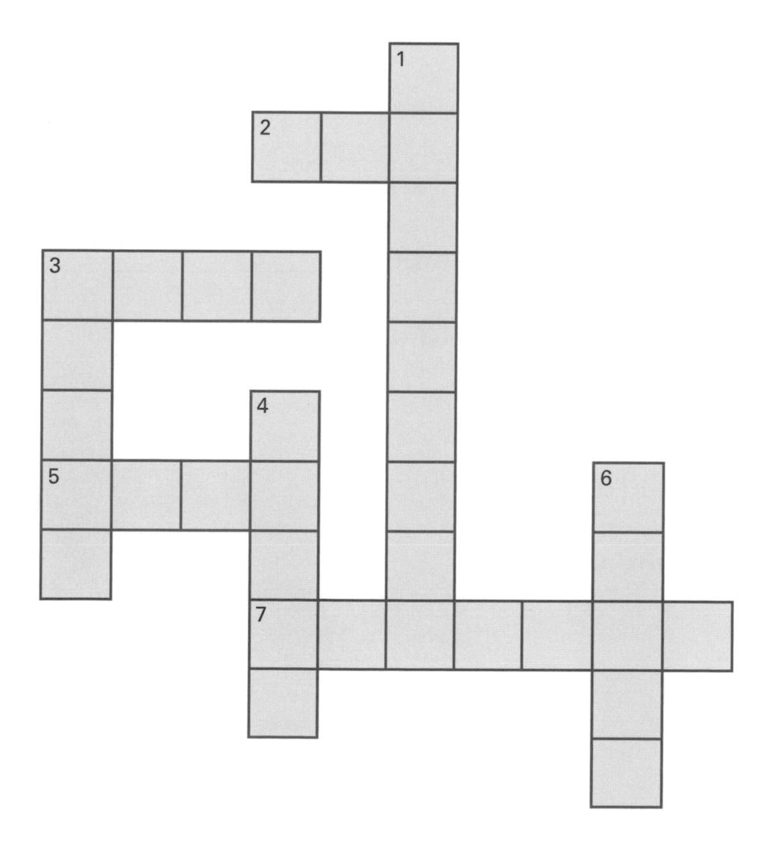

Blank Out!

FILL in the blanks with keywords.

aloud	allowed	creak	creek	hour
our	principal	principle	sighs	size

1. Henry had to practice piano for an ________________ before he could play basketball.
2. When she reeled it in, Lisa couldn't believe the ________________ of the fish.
3. Nate was ________________ to stay up later than his little brother.
4. Keely tiptoed, trying not to let the floor ________________.
5. We let out ________________ of relief when we heard there was no homework.
6. Stella went back to return the change as a matter of ________________.
7. Sammy kept his thoughts to himself rather than saying them ________________.
8. After the other team's third out, it will be ________________ turn at bat.
9. Our school's ________________ told us tomorrow is Silly Hat Day.
10. There has been so much rain that the ________________ may overflow.

Double Trouble

CIRCLE the keyword that completes each sentence.

1. Make sure to see the principle / principal for a late pass.
2. No one is allowed / aloud to come into my room without permission.
3. My mother always size / sighs if we leave our shoes in the middle of the floor.
4. The brownies took an hour / our to bake and only ten minutes to eat!
5. It was the principle / principal of the issue that bothered him.
6. We had to swim in our clothes because we forgot hour / our bathing suits!
7. Before the play, I practiced saying my lines aloud / allowed.
8. My uncle put some oil in the hinges so the door won't creek / creak.
9. A whale can be the sighs / size of a school bus.
10. The beavers were busy building a dam across the creek / creak.

Blank Out!

FILL IN the blanks with keywords.

aloud	allowed	creak	creek	hour
our	principal	principle	sighs	size

1. The ________________ tells how big or small something is.
2. This word describes something you believe is right. ________________
3. If it's your pizza *and* my pizza, it's ________________ pizza.
4. When you're permitted to do something, you're ________________ to do it.
5. When someone speaks above a whisper, he's speaking ________________.
6. The sounds of people exhaling loudly are called ________________.
7. A ________________ is smaller than a stream.
8. The head of a school is the ________________.
9. This word is the sound a rocking chair sometimes makes. ________________
10. It takes an ________________ for the minute hand to go around the clock once.

Check It!

Cut out the Check It! section on page 9, and see if you got the answers right.

Keywords

ad•dress[1]—uh-DREHS *verb* 1. to speak about an issue 2. to deal with

ad•dress[2]—A-drehs *noun* information that gives the location of someone's home or business or e-mail account

ex•cuse[1]—ihk-SKYOOS *noun* an explanation given to obtain forgiveness

ex•cuse[2]—ihk-SKYOOZ *verb* to overlook or forgive

proj•ect[1]—PRAH-jehkt *noun* a task

proj•ect[2]—pruh-JEHKT *verb* 1. to forecast 2. to jut out 3. to say loudly

re•cord[1]—REHK-erd *noun* 1. something official that preserves knowledge or history 2. best performance or greatest achievement

re•cord[2]—ri-KORD *verb* to make an audio, video, or written account of something

wound[1]—woond *noun* an injury

wound[2]—wownd *verb* 1. wrapped around something 2. changed direction

Check It!

Page 18

Read & Replace

1. project
2. address
3. record
4. wound
5. wound
6. excuse
7. project

Page 19

Homograph Hopscotch

1. excuse
2. record
3. wound

Page 20

Write It Right

1. wound
2. project
3. Excuse
4. address
5. record

Riddle: carpet

Page 21

Criss Cross

ACROSS	DOWN
2. address	1. record
3. project	4. record
7. project	5. excuse
8. wound	6. address
9. excuse	8. wound

Read & Replace

HOMOGRAPHS are words that have the same spelling but different meanings. They can sound alike or not, like *tear* that you cry and a *tear* in a page.

READ the list. FILL IN the blanks with keywords.

Seven Outrageous Excuses

Did you ever get invited somewhere you really didn't want to go? Just pick an excuse from this handy list!

1. I don't need to water the garden. I ________________ a big summer snow storm any minute.
2. I tried to run the errand for you, Mom, but an alien swiped the ________________.
3. I couldn't practice the piano because I was trying to set a ________________ for watching TV.
4. I'd eat those beets, but my allergy to red food makes me dizzy, and I might fall and ________________ myself.
5. Sorry I missed practice, but my brother ________________ me up with string and rolled me under the bed, and I was trapped until my mom found me.
6. You'll have to ________________ me—it's time for my daily chicken dance.
7. I wasn't yelling—I was just trying to ________________ so they could hear me on the moon.

Check It!

Page 22

Blank Out!

1. project
2. address
3. record
4. record
5. wound
6. excuse
7. address
8. wound
9. project
10. excuse

Page 23

Double Match Up

1. a, f
2. e, k
3. b, h
4. l, n
5. c, i
6. j, m
7. d, g

Page 24

Blank Out!

1. project
2. record
3. wound
4. address
5. excuse
6. address
7. Project
8. excuse
9. record
10. wound

Homograph Hopscotch

LOOK AT the definitions in each hopscotch board. FILL IN the matching keyword at the top of the board.

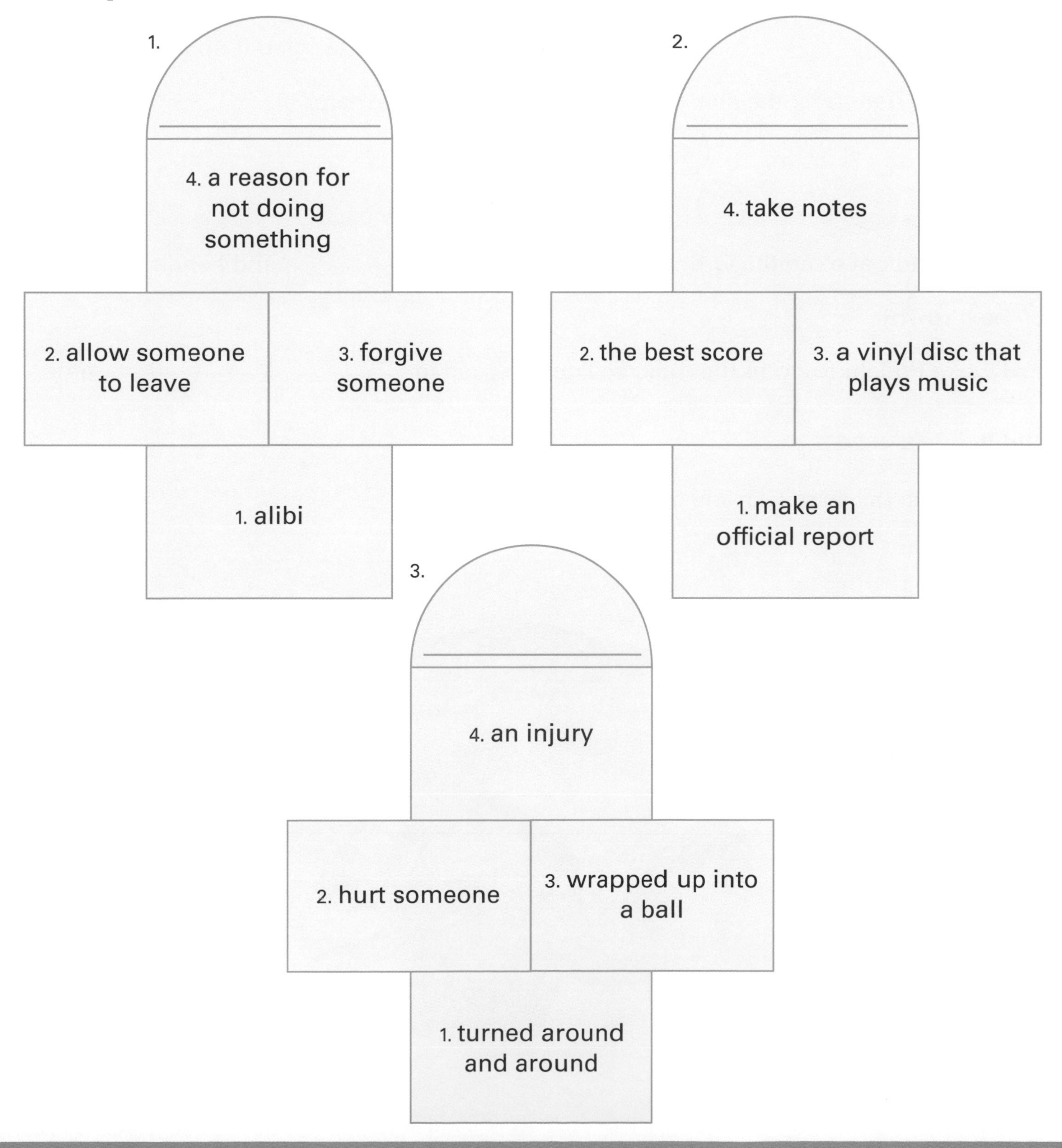

Write It Right

FILL IN the blanks by answering the clues with keywords. Then UNSCRAMBLE the letters in the circles to answer the riddle.

1. After I ___ ___ ___ ___ ___ the yarn into a ball, my cat tangled it up again!
2. My dad tried to fix the sink quickly but it turned into a major ◯ ___ ___ ___ ___ ___ ◯.
3. "___ ___ ◯ ___ ___ ◯ me!" I said after I burped.
4. My friend gave me the wrong ◯ ___ ___ ___ ___ ___ ___, and I ended up in the next town!
5. I woke up late to go to the mall, so I got dressed in ___ ___ ___ ___ ◯ ___ time.

Riddle

What goes up and down stairs without moving? ___ ___ ___ ___ ___ ___

Criss Cross

FILL IN the grid by answering the clues with keywords. Each keyword is used twice, with two different pronunciations.

ACROSS

2. What you write on an envelope
3. A big task
7. How to make yourself heard
8. Wrapped around
9. Let someone leave the dinner table

DOWN

1. Make an audio copy
4. The biggest or best achievement
5. "My homework flew out of the bus window."
6. Speak to a crowd
8. A bruise or cut

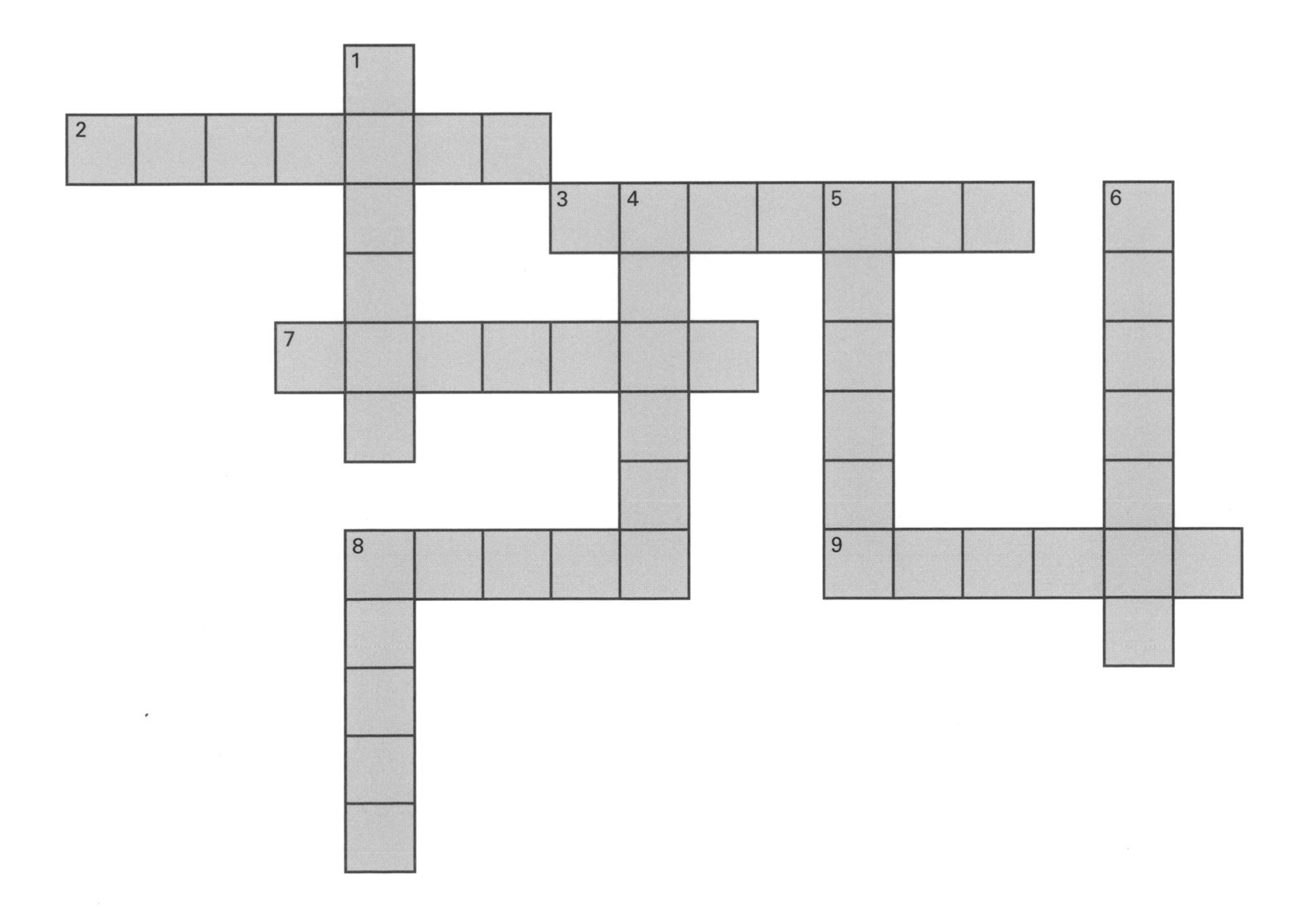

Blank Out!

FILL in the blanks with keywords.

address	excuse	project	record	wound

1. We decided to build a clubhouse for our next big ____________________.
2. Naomi got the ____________________ for the roller rink from the phone book.
3. Carlos broke the team ____________________ for goals scored in one game.
4. My mom keeps a chart to ____________________ the chores I do each week.
5. Madeline noticed a ____________________ on her dog's left paw.
6. There's no ____________________ for rude behavior!
7. The president is going to ____________________ the nation shortly.
8. When my sister was done flying her kite, she ____________________ the string on the spool.
9. Zack used a laptop to ____________________ the movie onto a screen.
10. My coach said he would ____________________ me from practice because I was sick.

Double Match Up

LOOK AT the words. FILL IN the blanks with the letters for both meanings of each word.

1. bark ______ ______
2. bow ______ ______
3. dove ______ ______
4. tear ______ ______
5. lead ______ ______
6. sewer ______ ______
7. wind ______ ______

a. the noise a dog makes
b. jumped head first
c. a kind of heavy metal
d. air that blows
e. loops formed when a ribbon is tied
f. outer surface of a tree
g. wrap something around
h. a bird of peace
i. to show the way
j. pipes in the ground that carry waste
k. a tool used when playing a violin
l. a drop formed when crying
m. someone who stitches
n. rip

Blank Out!

FILL in the blanks with keywords.

address	excuse	project	record	wound

1. Every time my sister cooks, the kitchen looks like a giant science ______________.
2. James is trying to set a world ______________ for the longest burp.
3. I took a header into a bush on my skateboard and got the grossest knee ______________ ever. Yes!
4. My uncle Ira is such a dork—his e-mail ______________ is hey@whatsamatteryou.com.
5. "The dog ate my homework" is the oldest ______________ in the world.
6. Quit making such a fuss—you're not giving the Gettysburg ______________ you know!
7. Poor Toby, everybody could hear his mother backstage telling him, "______________ your voice, Poopsie."
8. Well, ______________ me for living!
9. My dad has no idea how to work the DVR, so I have to ______________ all his faves for him.
10. Snoop wasn't laughing and joking with the rest of the team in the locker room because he's ______________ too tight.

Check It!

Cut out the Check It! section on page 17, and see if you got the answers right.

Just Right!

You've learned a lot of words so far. Are you ready to have some fun with them?

Synonyms may have similar meanings, but it's important to know which one is the right one to use in a situation. READ each sentence. Then CIRCLE the synonym that best fits the sentence.

1. Annie would rather go to the movie with a buddy / ally than by herself.
2. After a hard day at the office, my mom likes to loosen up / relax.
3. Over the summer, Nicki learned to dive / plunge off the board.
4. My brother won't enable / allow me to use his new baseball glove.
5. I hope we never stop / discontinue being friends.
6. It is polite / respectful to say "thank you" when you receive a gift.

Seesaw

LOOK AT the seesaws. WRITE a synonym on the level seesaws. Write an antonym on the slanted seesaws.

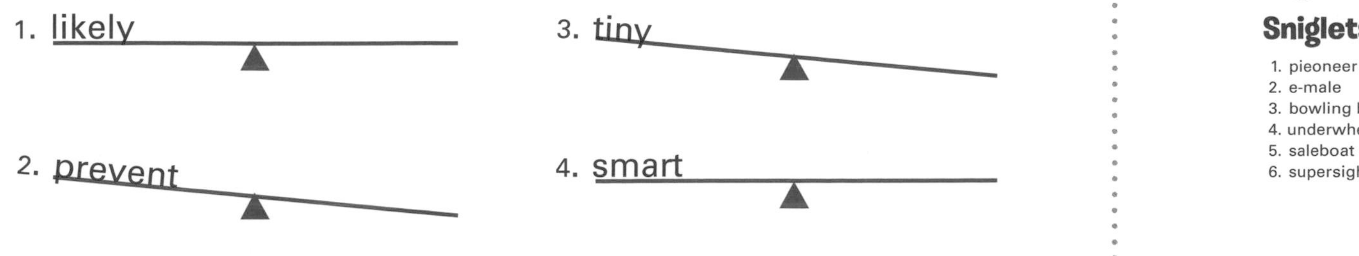

1. likely
2. prevent
3. tiny
4. smart

Check It!

Page 25

Just Right!

1. buddy
2. relax
3. dive
4. allow
5. stop
6. polite

Seesaw

1. probably
2. enable
3. immense
4. intelligent

Page 26

Word Search

Page 27

Fixer Upper

Glossary:
1. allowed
2. hour
3. principal
4. size
5. creek

Double Trouble

1. to speak to a crowd
2. an explanation for something you shouldn't have done
3. a task
4. to write an historic account
5. wrapped around

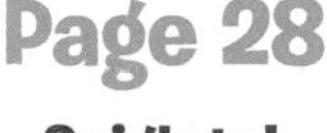

Page 28

Sniglets!

1. pieoneer
2. e-male
3. bowling bawl
4. underwhere
5. saleboat
6. supersighs

Word Search

CIRCLE all of the words in the word grid. Words go across, up, down, or diagonally.

amuse	polite	buddy	probably
discontinue	enable	immense	plunge
relax	climb	prevent	enemy
bore	rude	start	stupid
tiny	unlikely	stress	intelligent

Y	D	E	Y	T	E	P	R	E	Z	S	D	K	T	N
K	I	N	R	S	N	E	R	O	M	R	O	F	X	K
M	I	H	U	O	E	E	D	E	E	S	Y	R	O	T
T	Y	M	A	N	B	R	G	L	V	L	D	U	S	N
I	A	I	A	A	Y	W	A	I	B	E	W	T	S	D
M	O	B	H	I	A	X	E	A	L	Z	N	R	E	E
M	L	D	W	E	H	T	B	P	V	L	G	T	R	D
E	U	N	I	T	N	O	C	S	I	D	E	S	T	U
N	Q	U	X	P	R	E	T	I	L	O	P	T	S	R
S	N	S	H	P	U	Q	M	A	K	E	T	A	N	U
E	Y	N	U	M	Q	T	M	Y	M	G	J	R	S	I
K	D	B	U	D	P	C	S	V	V	N	H	T	V	J
H	A	U	N	L	I	K	E	L	Y	U	R	P	D	T
B	M	I	L	C	U	X	U	N	O	L	K	Z	A	X
B	U	D	D	Y	B	F	A	I	W	P	W	E	O	E

Fixer Upper

Our homophones have gotten all mixed up. READ the glossary. WRITE the keyword homophone that matches the definition.

Glossary

aloud: was given permission 1. ____________

our: unit of time; 60 minutes 2. ____________

principle: the main leader 3. ____________

sighs: how large something is height times width 4. ____________

creak: a small stream 5. ____________

Double Trouble

WRITE another meaning for each homograph.

address: where something is located OR 1. ____________

excuse: let someone go OR 2. ____________

project: speak loudly OR 3. ____________

record: the highest or best ever OR 4. ____________

wound: to injure OR 5. ____________

Sniglets!

Would you like to make up a new word? You can start by making up a *sniglet*. Sniglets are fun-sounding words that use pieces of existing words. Here are some homophone sniglets:

bowling bawl—a crying fit in a bowling alley
supersighs—loud exhaling sounds you make when you're frustrated
e-male—a computer note from a boy or man
pieoneer—one of the first people to eat a piece of pie
saleboat—a good price on a sea vessel
underwhere–missing undergarments

WRITE a sniglet from the list to complete each sentence.

1. When dessert was served, I volunteered to be the ________________.
2. Sarah was excited when Abel, captain of the football team, sent her an ________________.
3. After three gutter balls, my brother had a ________________.
4. All I have is ________________, so I can't get dressed and go with you.
5. My mother saved money by buying my dad a second-hand ________________ for his birthday.
6. You should've heard the waiter's ________________ when we changed our order for the third time.

Check It!

Cut out Check It! to see if you got the answers right.

Vive la France!

English is a funny language. Just when you think you've figured it out, there's something new to learn! That's because English is made up of many words from other languages. If you want to master those words, it can help to know where they came from.

Here are some French words that we've borrowed in English. MATCH each word to its synonym.

French words	English words
1. beau	a. coffee
2. bizarre	b. freedom
3. brochure	c. old
4. café	d. trait
5. ensemble	e. boyfriend
6. liberty	f. music group
7. quality	g. man's wig
8. toupée	h. town
9. village	i. flier
10. vintage	j. strange

Check It!

Page 29

Vive la France!

1. e
2. j
3. i
4. a
5. f
6. b
7. d
8. g
9. h
10. c

Page 30

Eat Your Words!

ITALY:
gelato, macaroni, spaghetti

JAPAN:
sushi, teriyaki, tofu

GERMANY:
frankfurter, sauerkraut, strudel

Page 31

Welcome to Spain!

1. d
2. g
3. i
4. b
5. j
6. a
7. f
8. c
9. h
10. e

Bonus:
1. distance
2. romantic
3. famous
4. demonstrate
5. problem

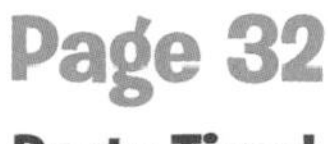

Page 32

Party Time!

FRANCE:
fête, soirée, Noël, Mardi Gras

GERMANY:
glockenspiel, Oktoberfest, polka

SPAIN:
Carnaval, fiesta, siesta, rodeo

Eat Your Words!

Did you have fun in France? Don't unpack your suitcase, because we're still traveling. And don't forget to pack your appetite.

Many foods from other countries have made their way to our kitchens... and into our dictionaries. Can you guess where these foods come from?

MATCH each food to its plate.

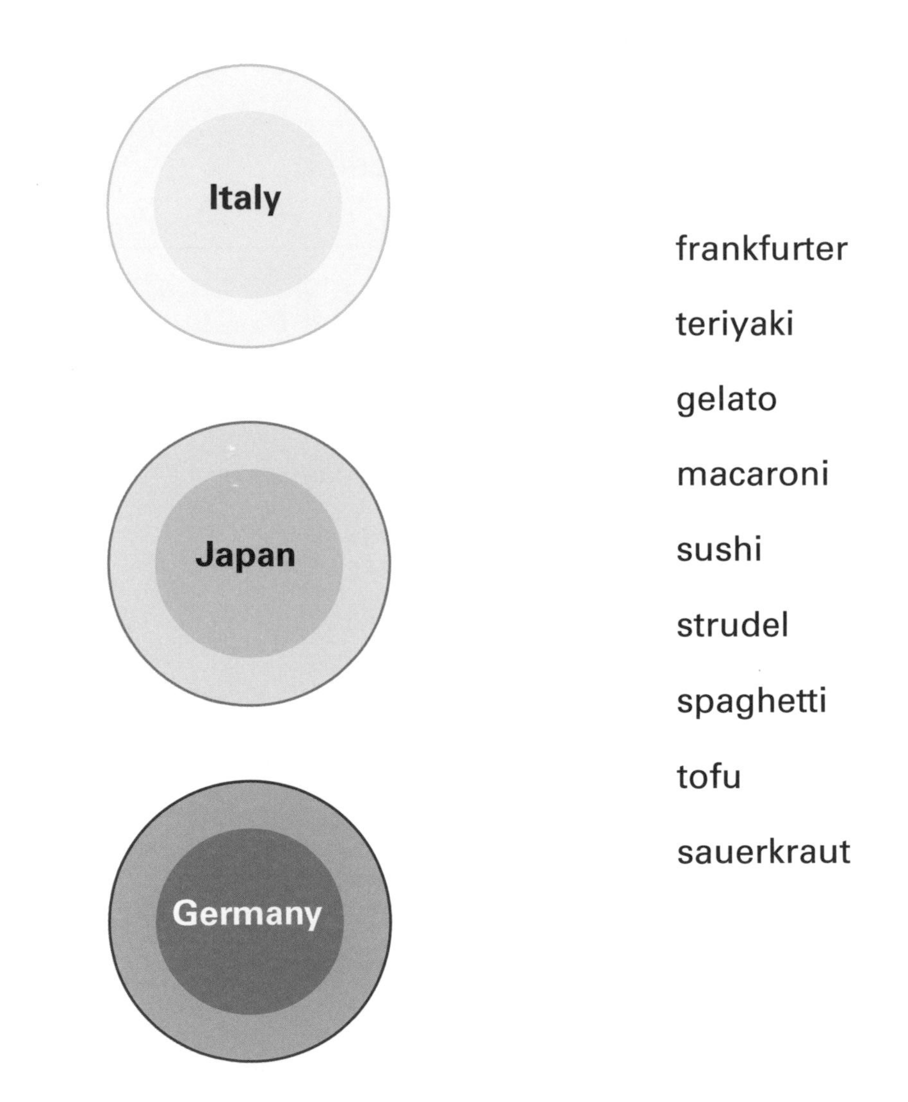

Welcome to Spain!

You may not know the language, but sometimes you can take a good guess. That's because many Spanish words will look very familiar to you.

LOOK AT the Spanish words. MATCH each one with an English word that looks similar.

1. aniversario	a. necessary
2. desperado	b. liquid
3. fantástico	c. ordinary
4. líquido	d. anniversary
5. magnífico	e. vacation
6. necesidad	f. obvious
7. obviamente	g. desperate
8. ordinario	h. rapid
9. rápido	i. fantastic
10. vacacion	j. magnificent

BONUS!

Write the English word for these familiar Spanish words.

1. distancia ______________________
2. romántico ______________________
3. famoso ______________________
4. demonstrar ______________________
5. probablemente ______________________

Party Time!

Time to celebrate all your new words! Cultures around the world have one thing in common—they like to have fun.

LOOK AT all the different celebratory words. MATCH them with the flags from the different countries.

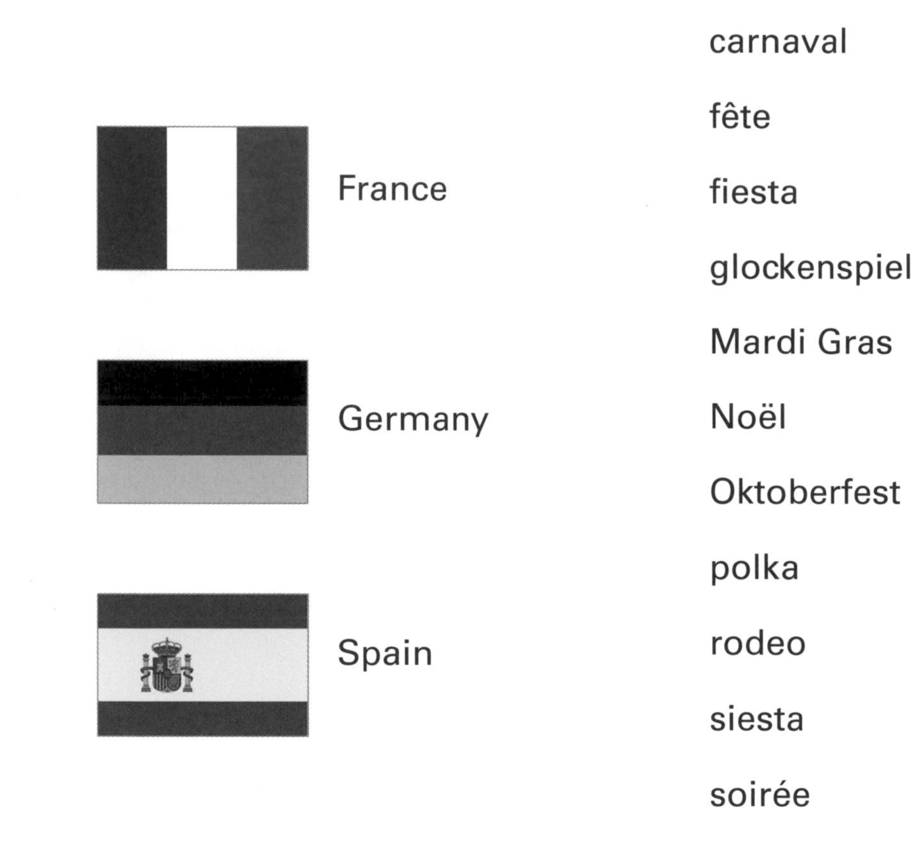

Keywords

im•po•lite—IHM-puh-LIT *adjective* 1. rude 2. lacking good manners

im•pos•si•ble—ihm-PAHS-uh-buhl *adjective* not able to occur

in•com•plete—ihn-kuhm-PLEET *adjective* not having all the necessary parts

in•cor•rect—ihn-kuh-REHKT *adjective* not having the right information

mis•be•have—MIHS-bih-HAYV *verb* to fail to act properly

mis•treat—mihs-TREET *verb* to deal with someone unfairly or cruelly

mis•un•der•stand—MIHS-uhn-der-STAND *verb* to fail to interpret something correctly

trans•con•ti•nen•tal—TRANS-kahn-tuh-NEHN-tuhl *adjective* crossing a continent

trans•late—TRANS-layt *verb* to convert one language to another

trans•port—TRANS-PORT *verb* to carry from one place to another

Check It!

Page 34

Match Up

impossible, i
incomplete, f
incorrect, e
misbehave, g
mistreat, a
misunderstand, d
transcontinental, b
translate, h
transport, c

Page 35

Read & Replace

1. impolite
2. misbehave
3. mistreat

Bonus:
"Not My Favorite"
"That's why you're not my fave."

Page 36

Petal Power

1. mis
2. in
3. trans
4. im

Page 37

Stack Up

IN: edible, exact, sane, humane
IM: perfect, mature
MIS: pronounce, inform
TRANS: atlantic, plant

Check It!

Page 38

Criss Cross

Across
3. mistreat
4. incomplete
6. translate
7. impossible

Down
1. transcontinental
2. impolite
4. incorrect
5. transport

Page 39

Blank Out!

1. transcontinental
2. incorrect
3. misbehave
4. impolite
5. mistreat
6. translate
7. misunderstand
8. incomplete
9. impossible
10. transport

Page 40

Blank Out!

1. incomplete
2. transport
3. impolite
4. misbehave
5. misunderstand
6. incorrect
7. impossible
8. mistreat
9. transcontinental
10. translate

Match Up

A PREFIX is a group of letters that comes at the beginning of a word. Each prefix has its own meaning. When you know the meaning of the prefix, you can often figure out the meaning of the word.

MATCH the prefixes in the box to the roots. WRITE each word and then MATCH it to its definition.

HINT: You can use each prefix more than once.

in-/im- = not　　mis- = bad　　trans- = across

port ____________________ ______
understand ____________________ ______
late ____________________ ______
continental ____________________ ______
correct ____________________ ______
possible ____________________ ______
treat ____________________ ______
behave ____________________ ______
complete ____________________ ______

Definitions:

a. to deal with someone unfairly or cruelly
b. crossing a continent
c. to carry from one place to another
d. to fail to interpret something correctly
e. not having the right information
f. not having all the necessary parts
g. to fail to act properly
h. to convert one language to another
i. not able to occur

Read & Replace

READ the poem. Then FILL IN the blanks in the second poem using keywords to give the poem the opposite meaning.

My Favorite

You're ever so **polite**,

And you always **behave**,

You know how to **treat** me.

That's why you're my fave!

My Favorite

You're ever so 1 ______________________,

And you always 2 ______________________,

You know how to 3 ______________________ me.

That's why you're my fave!

BONUS!

For the second poem, what word do you need to add to the last line to make it make sense? Add that extra word to the title and last line.

Petal Power

READ the roots on the petals around each flower. FILL IN the center of each flower with a prefix that could go with all of its roots.

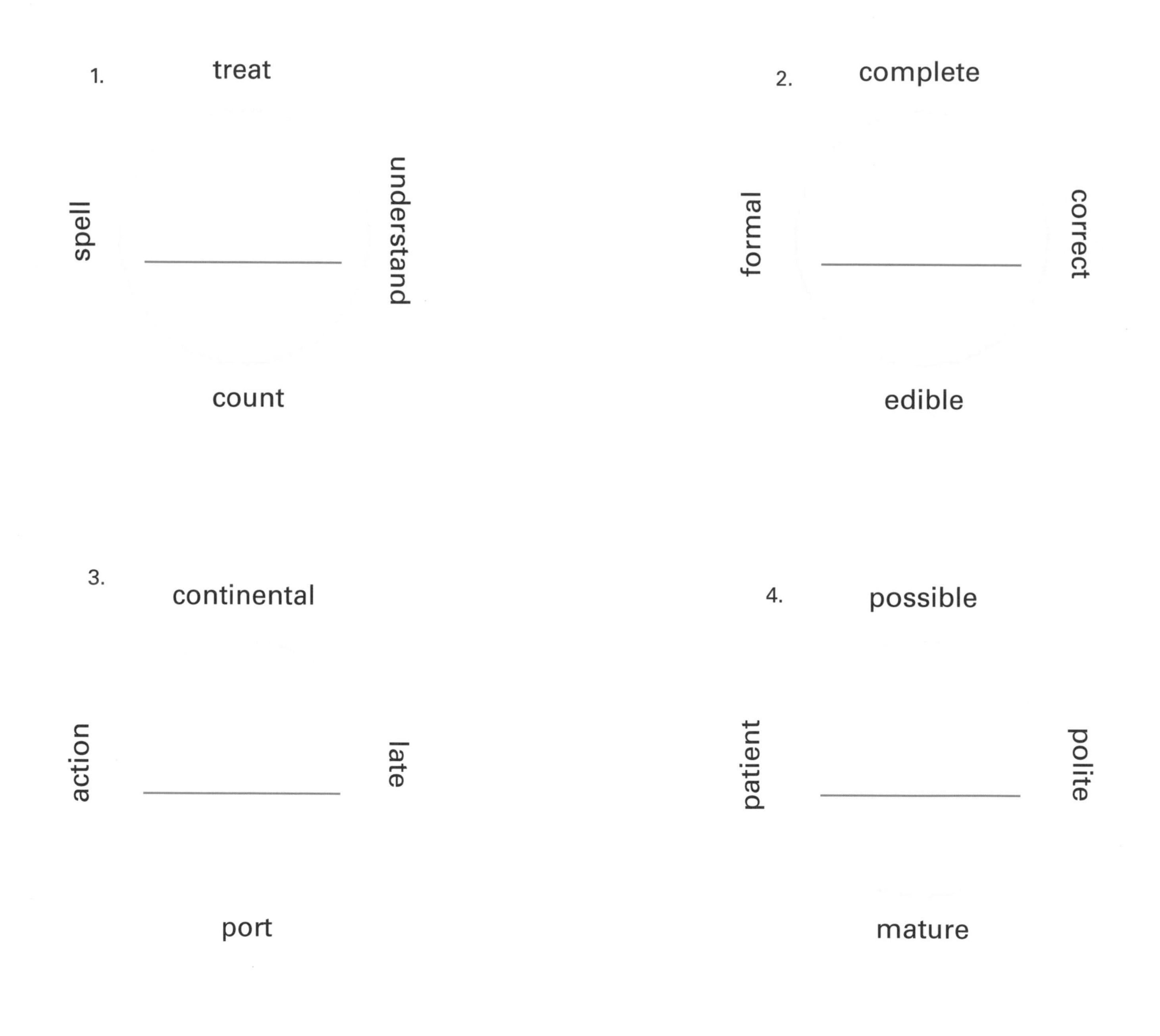

Stack Up

LOOK AT the root words in the box. MATCH them with prefixes to make new words. WRITE the new words under each prefix.

sane	pronounce	exact	plant	mature
humane	atlantic	perfect	inform	edible

in-

____

____

____

____

im-

____

____

mis-

____

____

trans-

____

____

Criss Cross

FILL IN the grid by answering the clues with keywords.

ACROSS

3. Handle someone badly
4. Not finished
6. Change words to a different language
7. Can't be done

DOWN

1. From coast to coast
2. Rude
4. Wrong
5. Carry

Blank Out!

FILL IN the blanks with keywords.

1. The ____________________ railroad runs across the entire country.
2. Lily said she thought I liked Bryan, but I told her she was totally ____________________.
3. If we leave our dog alone too long, he tends to ____________________.
4. I said I liked her gift because I didn't want to be ____________________.
5. People who ____________________ animals should not be allowed to have pets.
6. The story was in Spanish so I got my friend to ____________________ it.
7. If you don't listen closely, you might ____________________ the directions.
8. The jigsaw puzzle was ____________________ because our dog ate a piece!
9. My sister packed so much that it was ____________________ to close her suitcase.
10. We needed a big truck and some movers to ____________________ the piano to our house.

Blank Out!

FILL IN the blanks with keywords.

1. The story is incomplete because the last few pages are ____________________.
2. You ____________________ something to get it from one place to another.
3. Someone who doesn't have good manners is ____________________.
4. Some kids ____________________ when their parents are out.
5. A person who isn't listening closely might ____________________.
6. A wrong answer is ____________________.
7. Something that just can't be done is ____________________.
8. You can't borrow my clothes anymore because you always ____________________ them.
9. A highway stretching coast to coast is ____________________.
10. To read a book in another language, you might ____________________ it.

Keywords

an•ti•bac•te•ri•al—AN-tee- bak-TEER-ee-uhl *adjective* active in killing germs

an•ti•slav•er•y—AN-tee-SLAY-vuh-ree *adjective* against the practice of owning people

an•ti•so•cial—AN-tee-SOH-shuhl *adjective* not wanting to be with other people

in•ter•na•tion•al—IHN-ter-NASH-uh-nuhl *adjective* between two or more countries

in•ter•sect—IHN-ter-SEHKT *verb* 1. to divide something by going across it 2. to cross or overlap

in•ter•state—IHN-ter-STAYT *adjective* between two or more states

mul•ti•col•ored—MUHL-tih-KUHL-erd *adjective* having many hues

mul•ti•cul•tur•al—MUHL-tee-KUHL-cher-uhl *adjective* reflecting many different customs and backgrounds

mul•ti•mil•lion•aire—MUHL-tee-MIHL-yuh-NEHR *noun* someone a person who has millions of dollars

mul•ti•pur•pose—MUHL-tee-PER-puhs *adjective* having more than one use

Check It!

Page 42

Read & Replace

1. multipurpose
2. intersect
3. interstate
4. multimillionaire
5. antibacterial
6. antisocial
7. multicolored
8. international
9. multicultural
10. antislavery

Page 43

Petal Power

1. inter
2. anti
3. multi

Bonus:
predawn
pregame
preheat
preteen

Page 44

Tic-Tac-Toe

1. war, gravity, bodies
2. galactic, weave, action
3. layer, task, channel

antibodies
anticlimax
antigravity
antivenom
antiwar

interaction
interchangeable
intergalactic
international
interweave

multichannel
multifaceted
multilayer
multilingual
multitask

Read & Replace

READ the newspaper story. FILL IN the blanks with keywords.

HINT: Make sure to read the whole story first.

anti- = against   *inter- = among or between*   *multi = many or much*

INVENTION CONVENTION

This year's Invention Convention entries were zany. Michael Finch created the "Umbre-Light-Chair," a 1 ________________ item—an umbrella, flashlight, and folding chair. He explained that the three purposes would 2 ________________ if you wanted to sit on the beach on a rainy night. "I hope to win the local convention and go to the 3 ________________ competition, he said. "One day I'll be a 4 ________________!"

Lydia Nelson is a germ freak. She created 5 ________________ lip balm. "Any germs that touch your lips are killed before they enter your mouth." She added that it's best to avoid large groups of people, "without being too 6 ________________."

First prize went to Alex Price. He created a 7 ________________ symbol with different paints. "I would like my design to become an 8 ________________ symbol of respect so people can honor our 9 ________________ world." He added, "I read about the efforts people made during the 10 ________________ movement to gain freedom. This is something we can use today."

Check It!

Page 45

Criss Cross

Across
3. intersect
6. antislavery
7. antisocial

Down
1. multicultural
2. interstate
4. international
5. multicolored

Page 46

Blank Out!

1. multimillionaire
2. international
3. multicultural
4. antislavery
5. antibacterial
6. multipurpose
7. intersect
8. multicolored
9. antisocial
10. interstate

Page 47

It's Puzzling!

antifreeze
antiwar
intercom
interlocked
interview
multiethnic
multiplex
multiplication

Page 48

Blank Out!

1. interstate
2. multicolored
3. antisocial
4. multimillionaire
5. antibacterial
6. antislavery
7. multicultural
8. international
9. intersect
10. multipurpose

Petal Power

READ the roots on the petals around each flower. FILL IN the center of each flower with a prefix that could go with all of its roots.

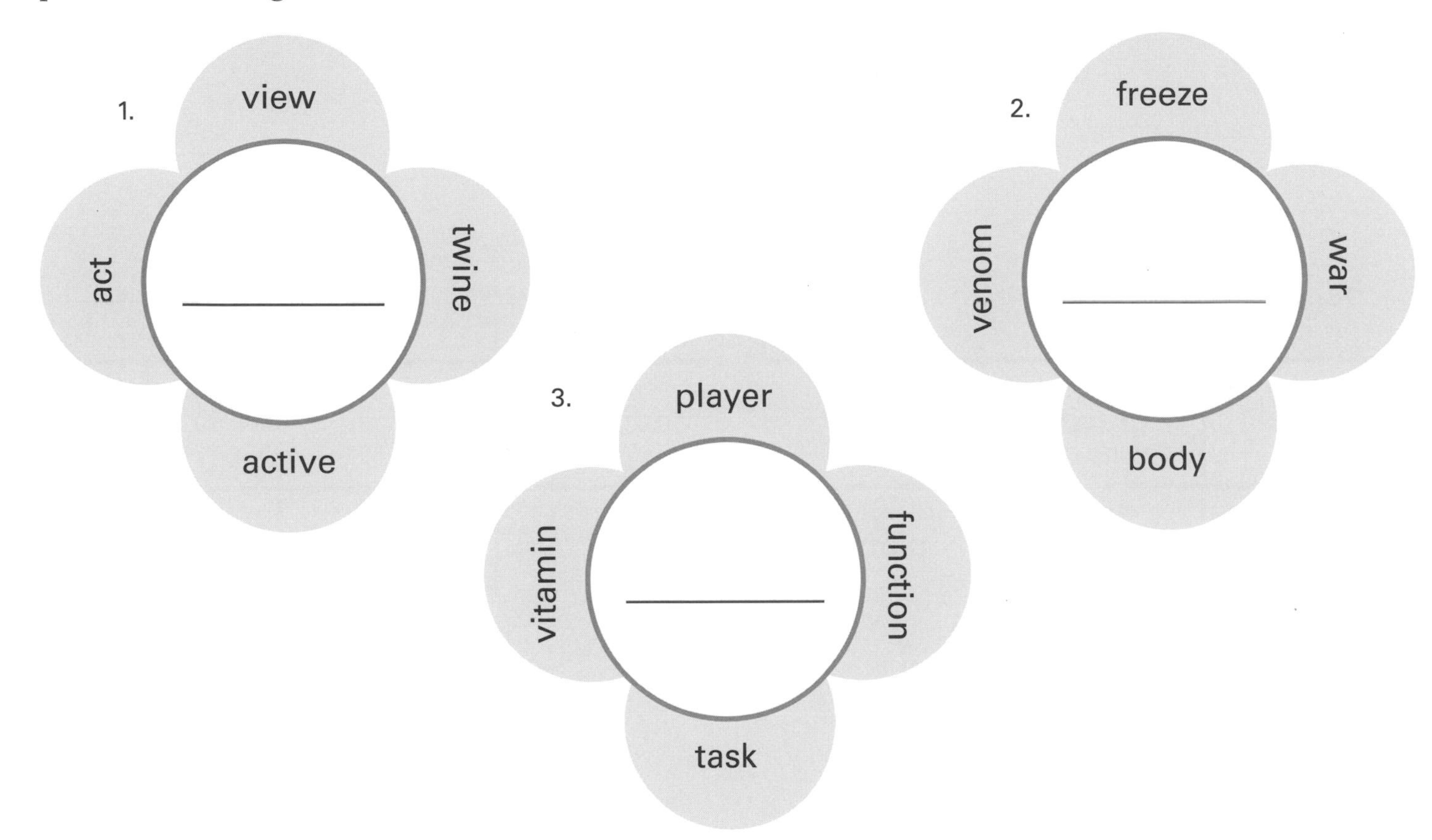

BONUS!

Now you try it! The prefix in the middle of this flower means *before*. FILL IN the petals with root words that go with the center. One petal is filled in for you!

bend	dawn	game	teen
circle	feet	heat	obey

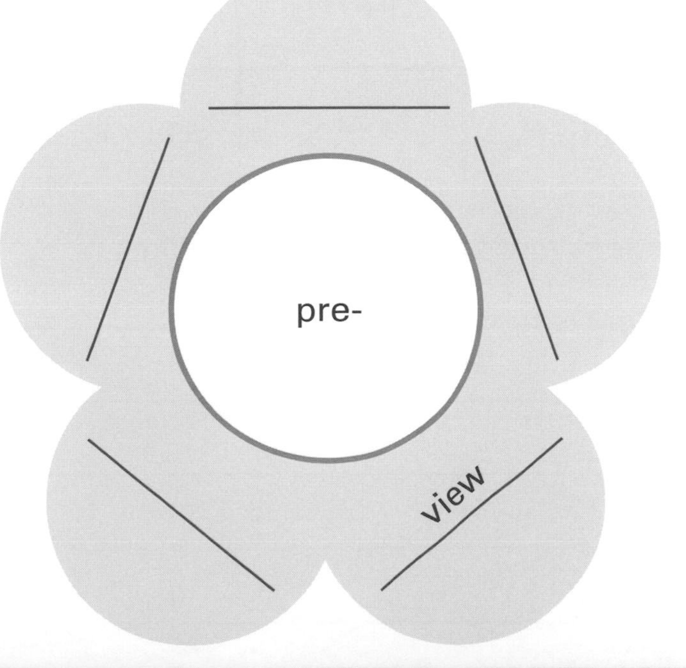

Tic-Tac-Toe

PLAY Tic-tac-toe with prefixes. CIRCLE any root that could be used with the prefix in blue. PUT an X through any word that could not be used with the prefix. When you find three X's or O's in a row, you're a winner! The line can go across, down, or diagonally. When you're done, make a list of all the new words.

HINT: If you find a word you don't know, check a dictionary or thesaurus.

1. anti

paper	war	happy
index	gravity	climax
venom	bodies	planets

2. inter

changeable	car	action
addition	weave	national
galactic	spoke	mud

3. multi

layer	green	porch
task	travel	lingual
channel	faceted	novel

Other Words Created with Prefixes

Criss Cross

FILL IN the grid by answering the clues with keywords.

ACROSS

3. Divide by running across something
6. Against the ownership of people
7. Not interested in hanging out

DOWN

1. From many different backgrounds
2. The champions traveled 200 miles to an ____ competition.
4. Flights to other countries depart from the ____ terminal.
5. Not just one hue

Blank Out!

FILL IN the blanks with keywords.

1. The inventor of the Pet Rock probably became a ________________.
2. With their new hit song in many different languages, the band became an ________ sensation.
3. My friends and I prepared a ________________ feast with foods from different backgrounds.
4. Harriet Tubman was a famous leader of the ________________ movement.
5. Mary is such a germ freak that she applies ________________ gel every time she shakes hands with someone.
6. Zach's crazy ________________ tool had a screwdriver, file, scissors, nail clippers, tongue scraper, and ear wax remover!
7. On a globe, lines of latitude and longitude ________________ each other.
8. She took out all her markers to make a ________________ poster.
9. Alison didn't want to go to the party because she was feeling ________________.
10. To get from Pennsylvania to Ohio, we took an ________________ highway.

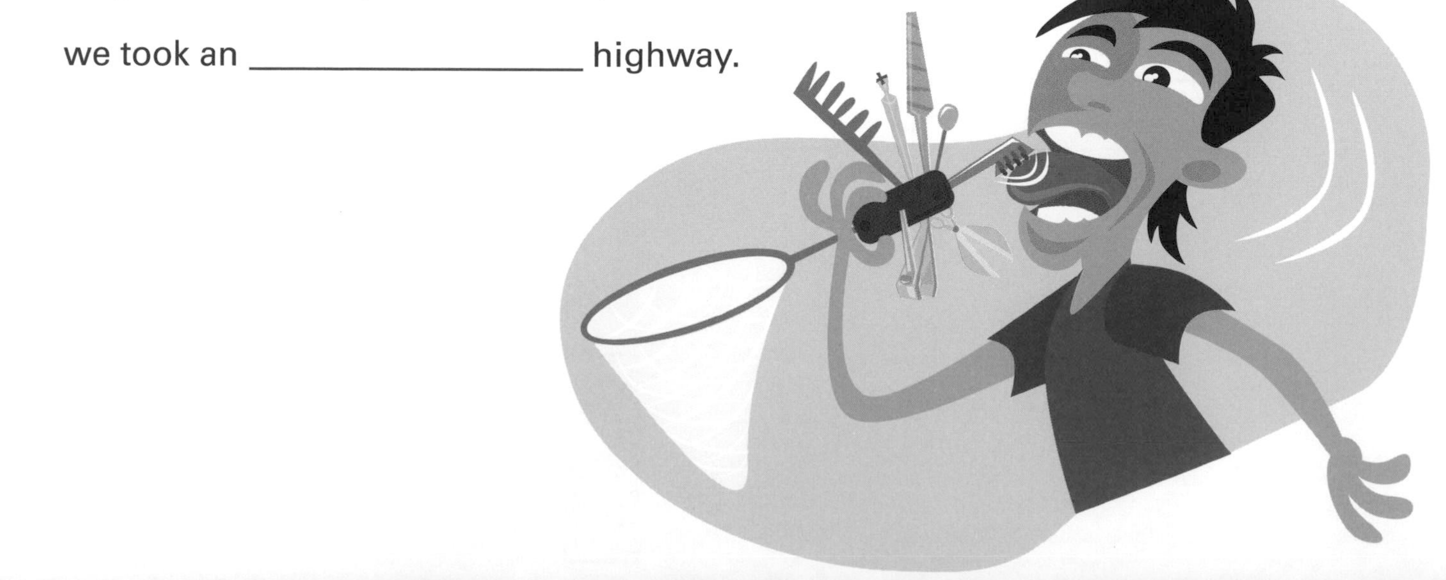

It's Puzzling!

MATCH each prefix to a root. Then WRITE the words in the blanks.

HINT: You can use the same prefix more than once.

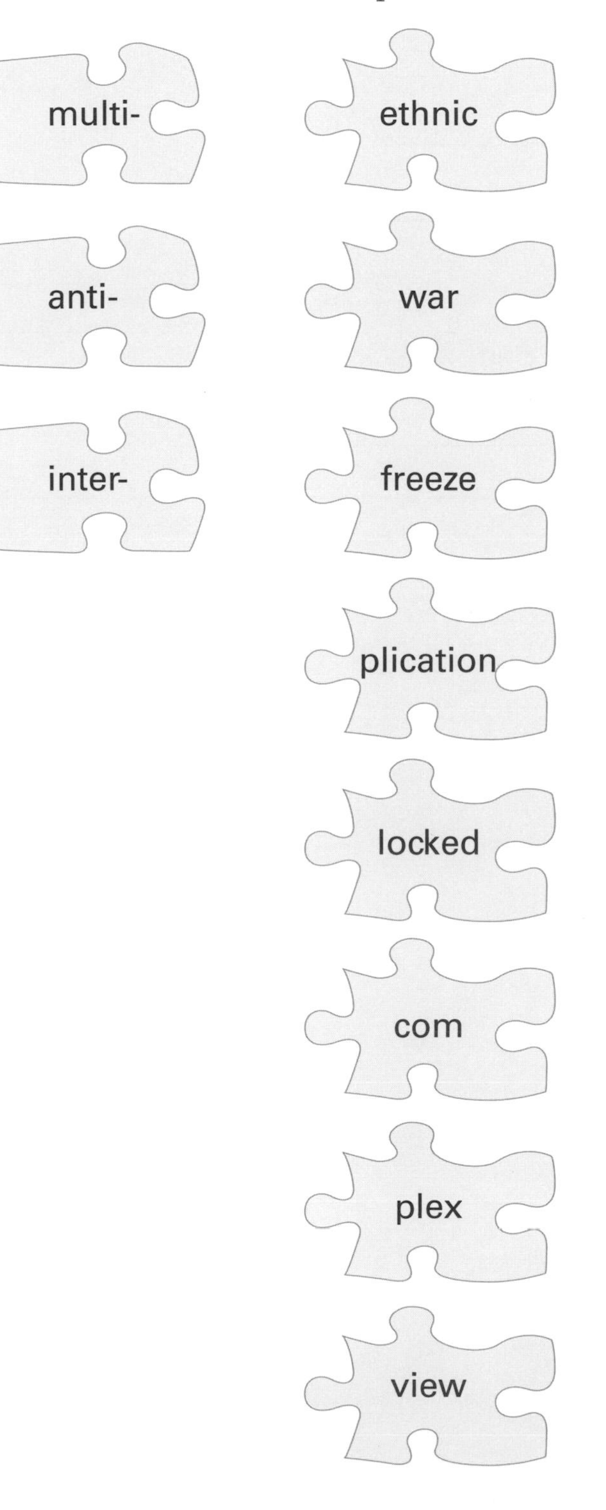

____

____

____

____

____

____

____

____

Blank Out!

FILL IN the blanks with keywords.

1. When we left on vacation, we took the ________________ highway to the airport.
2. A rainbow is ________________.
3. Someone who prefers to be alone is ________________.
4. A person with loads of money may be a ________________.
5. Something that kills germs is ________________.
6. A movement against some people owning other people is ________________.
7. A group with people from many backgrounds is ________________.
8. A world's fair is an ________________ event.
9. Two lines that cross each other ________________.
10. Something that has many uses is ________________.

Keywords

bi•an•nu •al—bi-AN-yoo-uhl *adjective* occurring twice a year

bi•cy•cle—BI-sihk-uhl *noun* a two-wheeled vehicle

bin•oc•u•lars—buh-NOK-yuh-lerz *noun* a magnifying device with two lenses for seeing faraway objects

tri•an•gle—TRI-ang-guhl *noun* a shape with three sides

tri•ath•lon—tri-ATH-luhn *noun* a sports event with three different activities

trip•lets—TRIHP-lihts *noun* three children born at the same birth

tri•pod—TRI-pahd *noun* a three-legged stand

u•ni•corn—YOO-nih-korn *noun* an imaginary horse-like animal with a single horn

u•ni•cy•cle—YOO-nih-SI-kuhl *noun* a one-wheeled vehicle

u•ni•verse—YOO-nuh-vers *noun* all planets, space, and matter and energy in one whole

Check It!

Page 50

Read & Replace

1. unicycle
2. bicycle
3. binoculars
4. unicorn
5. triplets
6. triangle
7. tripod
8. triathlon
9. biannual
10. universe

Page 51

1, 2, 3 Stack Up!

1. unicorn, unicycle, universe
2. bicycle, binoculars, biannual
3. triangle, tripod, triathlon, triplets

Page 52

Tic-Tac-Toe

1. uniform, unibrow, unicolor
2. bipolar, biweekly, bimonthly
3. triathlete, tricolor, tricycle

uniform
unibrow
unicorn
unicolor
unidirectional

bifocals
bilevel
bipolar
biweekly
bimonthly

trifocal
trifold
triathlete
tricolor
tricycle

Read & Replace

Some prefixes just add a number to the root word. A *uni*cycle has one wheel. A *bi*cycle has two wheels. And a *tri*cycle has three wheels.

READ the story. FILL IN the blanks with keywords.

Prefix Meanings: *uni- = one* *bi- = two* *tri- = three*

unicorn	unicycle	universe	bicycle
binoculars	binannual	triangle	tripod
triathlon	triplets		

Every year my town has a festival. This year was the best ever. A clown juggled while riding a 1 ____________. I can't ride one even when I'm *not* juggling! It was even more amazing to see an elephant riding a 2 ____________! I looked at it up-close through my 3 ____________. A horse was dressed in a costume as a 4 ____________. Three acrobats were identical 5 ____________. They swung from a giant 6 ____________. A photographer had a camera on a 7 ____________. You could get your picture taken behind silly cardboard cutouts. Afterwards, kids and grown-ups could join in a 8 ____________ contest with wheelbarrow races, sack hops, and leapfrog! It only happens once a year, but I wish it were a 9 ____________ event. It's the best festival in the 10 ____________!

Check It!

Page 53

Criss Cross

ACROSS
5. unicycle
6. tripod
7. triplets

DOWN
1. bicycle
2. binoculars
3. unicorn
4. triangle
5. universe

Page 54

Blank Out!

1. bicycle
2. triathlon
3. biannual
4. unicorn
5. triangle
6. universe
7. binoculars
8. unicycle
9. Tripod
10. triplets

Page 55

Name It!

1. tricorn
2. uninostril
3. bilight

Page 56

Blank Out!

1. Binoculars
2. triangle
3. bicycle
4. unicycle
5. triathlon
6. universe
7. biannual
8. unicorn
9. tripod
10. triplets

1, 2, 3 Stack Up!

READ the definitions. Then WRITE the keyword under the number that matches its prefix.

An animal with one horn

Happening twice a year

A stand with three legs

A set of three babies born at the same time

The whole world and beyond

A vehicle with two wheels

A shape with three angles

A magnifying device with two lenses

A sports event with three different activities

A vehicle with one wheel

1	2	3
______	______	______
______	______	______
______	______	______
		______

Tic-Tac-Toe

PLAY Tic-tac-toe with prefixes. CIRCLE any root that could be used with the prefix in blue. PUT an X through any word that could not be used with the prefix. When you find three Xs or Os in a row, you're a winner! The line can go across, down, or diagonally. When you're done, make a list of all the words.

HINT: If you find a word you don't know, check a dictionary or thesaurus.

1. uni

week	month	corn
form	brow	color
stream	directional	change

2. bi

polar	tail	pack
level	weekly	grain
cell	focals	monthly

3. tri

focal	athlete	student
notes	color	fold
elbow	cycle	phone

Other Words Created with Prefixes

Criss Cross

FILL IN the grid by answering the clues with keywords.

ACROSS

5. Bicycle minus one wheel
6. Something steady to put your camera on
7. One more than twins

DOWN

1. A unicycle plus one wheel
2. What you might use to watch birds
3. Mythical one-horned creature
4. A simple instrument to ding in music class
5. Something greater than our galaxy

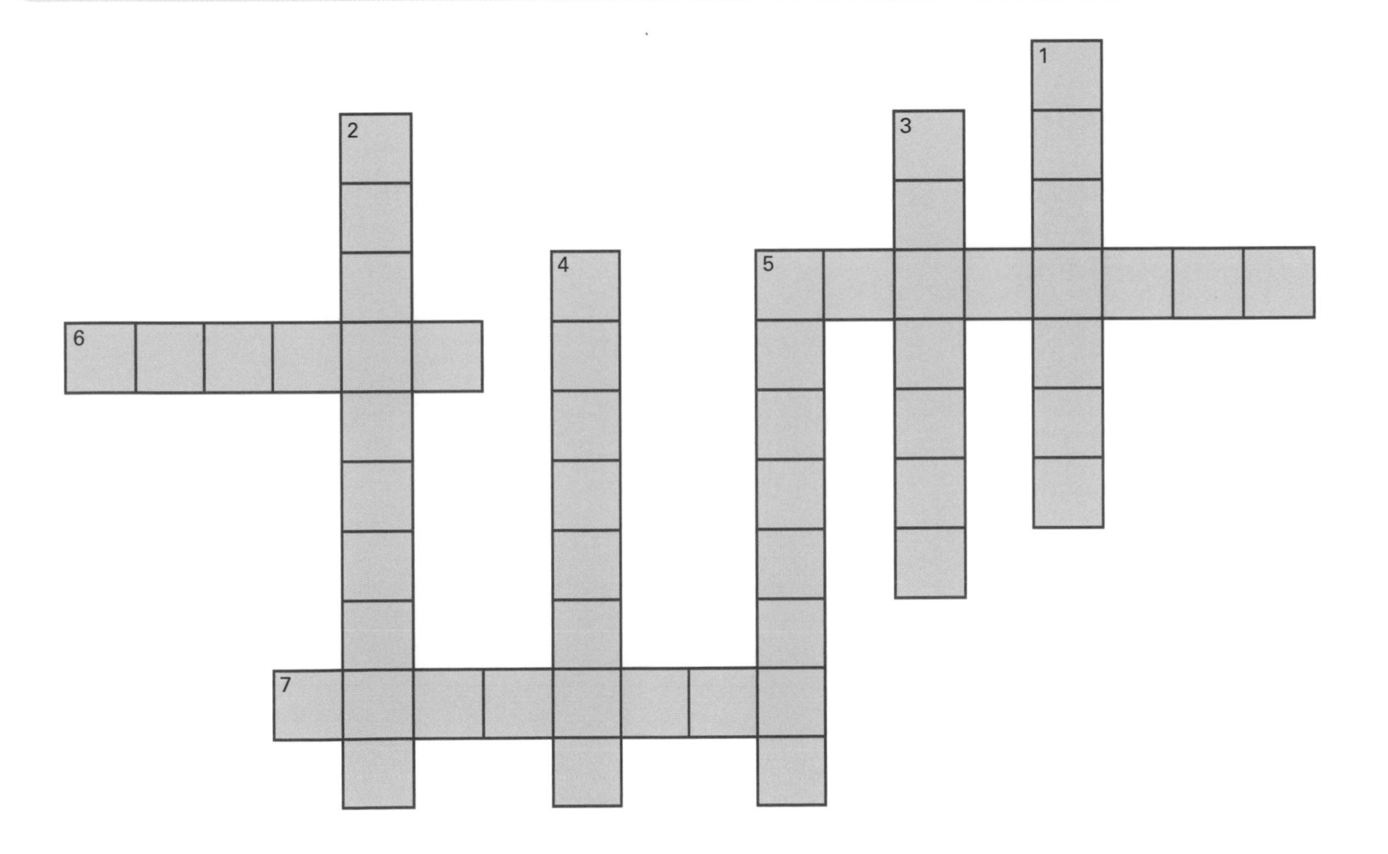

Blank Out!

FILL IN the blanks with keywords.

1. Riding a __________________ is great exercise.
2. Dad was training to push a shopping cart up a hill and balance a dozen eggs on his head for the grocery __________________.
3. Our neighborhood throws a __________________ block party in the spring and fall.
4. My little sister won't go anywhere without her stuffed __________________.
5. A slice of pizza is shaped like a __________________.
6. Each planet is one little speck in the __________________.
7. I crouched by the window and used __________________ to try to catch the newspaper thief.
8. For the talent show, Tim rode his __________________ while balancing his cat George on one hand.
9. Our dog only has three legs, so we named him __________________.
10. The __________________ played tricks on their teachers by switching places.

Name It!

LOOK AT the pictures. INVENT a word that describes the picture, using the prefixes *uni-*, *bi-*, and *tri-*. WRITE the word and define it.

1. ______________________________

____

____

2. ______________________________

____

____

3. ______________________________

____

____

Blank Out!

FILL IN the blanks with keywords.

1. ____________________ can help you watch a baseball game from the bleachers.
2. A ____________________ is a shape with three sides.
3. A ____________________ is an environmentally friendly way to get around.
4. A clown sometimes rides a ____________________.
5. A ____________________ can be an event with biking, running, and swimming.
6. The ____________________ is even bigger than the solar system.
7. This word describes something that happens twice a year. ____________________
8. A ____________________ is a mythical creature.
9. A three-legged stool is a ____________________.
10. Three babies delivered at the same birth are ____________________.

Keywords

cer•tain•ty—SER-tuhn-tee *noun* the state of being sure

con•struc•tion—kuhn-STRUHK-shuhn *noun* the process of building

cre•a•tive—kree-AY-tihv *adjective* capable of making or imagining new things

de•ci•sive—dih-SI-sihv *adjective* having the power to make firm decisions

ed•u•ca•tion—EH-juh-KAY-shuhn *noun* the act of learning or teaching

ex•plo•sion—ihk-SPLOH-shuhn *noun* a sudden burst, often loud or violent

i•mag•i•na•tion—ih-MAJ-uh-NAY-shuhn *noun* the ability of the mind to create

in•for•ma•tion—IHN-fer-MAY-shuhn *noun* facts or knowledge gained from any source

per•mis•sion—per-MIH-shuhn *noun* the act of allowing

sim•i•lar•i•ty—SIHM-uh-LAR-ih-tee *noun* the state of having a lot in common

Check It!

Page 58

Read & Replace

1. construction
2. imagination
3. information
4. creative
5. similarity
6. explosion
7. permission
8. decisive
9. certainty
10. education

Page 59

Suffix Hopscotch

1. -ion
2. -ity
3. -ive

Page 60

Match Up

1. deletion
2. royalty
3. conversation
4. revision
5. frailty

Page 61

Criss Cross

ACROSS	DOWN
4. construction	1. education
7. imagination	2. similarity
8. permission	3. creative
	5. decisive
	6. explosion

Check It!

Page 62

Blank Out!

1. education
2. decisive
3. construction
4. information
5. explosion
6. certainty
7. permission
8. creative
9. similarity
10. imagination

Page 63

Chopping Block

1. combine
2. invade
3. tense
4. loyal
5. migrate
6. opt
7. illustrate
8. invade
9. add
10. divide

Page 64

Blank Out!

1. permission
2. Construction
3. explosion
4. decisive
5. similarity
6. creative
7. imagination
8. information
9. Certainty
10. Education

Read & Replace

READ the diary entry. FILL IN the blanks with keywords.

Stadium Blast!

Today they started 1 ________________ on the new baseball stadium. I've been to the old arena many times. The idea of building an entirely new one boggled my 2 ________________. How would they do it? I found some 3 ________________ online. The designs for the new stadium are very 4 ________________. There will be a giant dolphin-shaped scoreboard past the outfield fence. There will be brand-new, fancy dugouts. The only 5 ________________ will be the field!

My dad told me that they were going to start by demolishing the old structure. They were actually going to set off an 6 ________________! Dad said that people had 7 ________________ to watch from a safe distance. He asked if I wanted to go. Naturally, I replied with a 8 ________________ YES!

Even though we were across the street, the blast was deafening. The buildings around us shook. The stadium came crashing down. One thing I can say with 9 ________________—it was an 10 ________________!

Suffix Hopscotch

LOOK AT the root words in each hopscotch board. FILL IN the matching suffix at the top of the board.

HINT: Sometimes you drop or change a letter from the root word when you add the suffix.

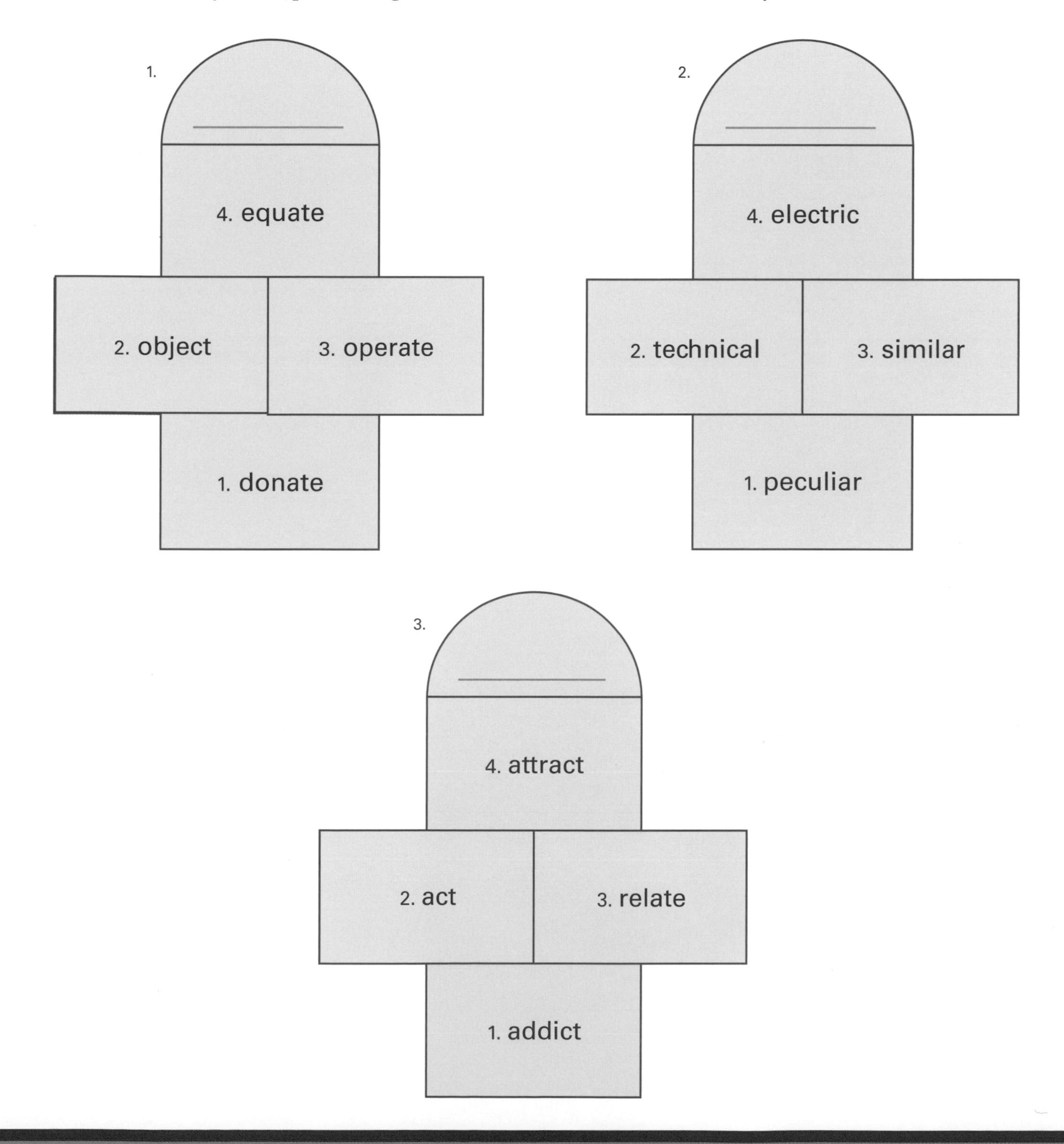

Match Up

MATCH each root to a suffix. Then WRITE the word next to its definition.

HINT: Sometimes you drop or change a letter from the root word when you add the suffix.

Root	Suffix
delete	-ty
royal	-ion
converse	-ion
revise	-ty
frail	-ation

	Word	Definition
1.	____________________	the act of removing something
2.	____________________	kings, queens, and their relatives
3.	____________________	discussion
4.	____________________	a changed form of something
5.	____________________	the state of being weak or delicate

Criss Cross

FILL IN the grid by answering the clues with keywords.

ACROSS

4. Describes a zone where people wear hardhats
7. Something you need to think up a great plan
8. The go-ahead

DOWN

1. Something you get from school
2. A likeness or resemblance
3. Comes up with zany ideas
5. No trouble choosing
6. Something that goes BOOM!

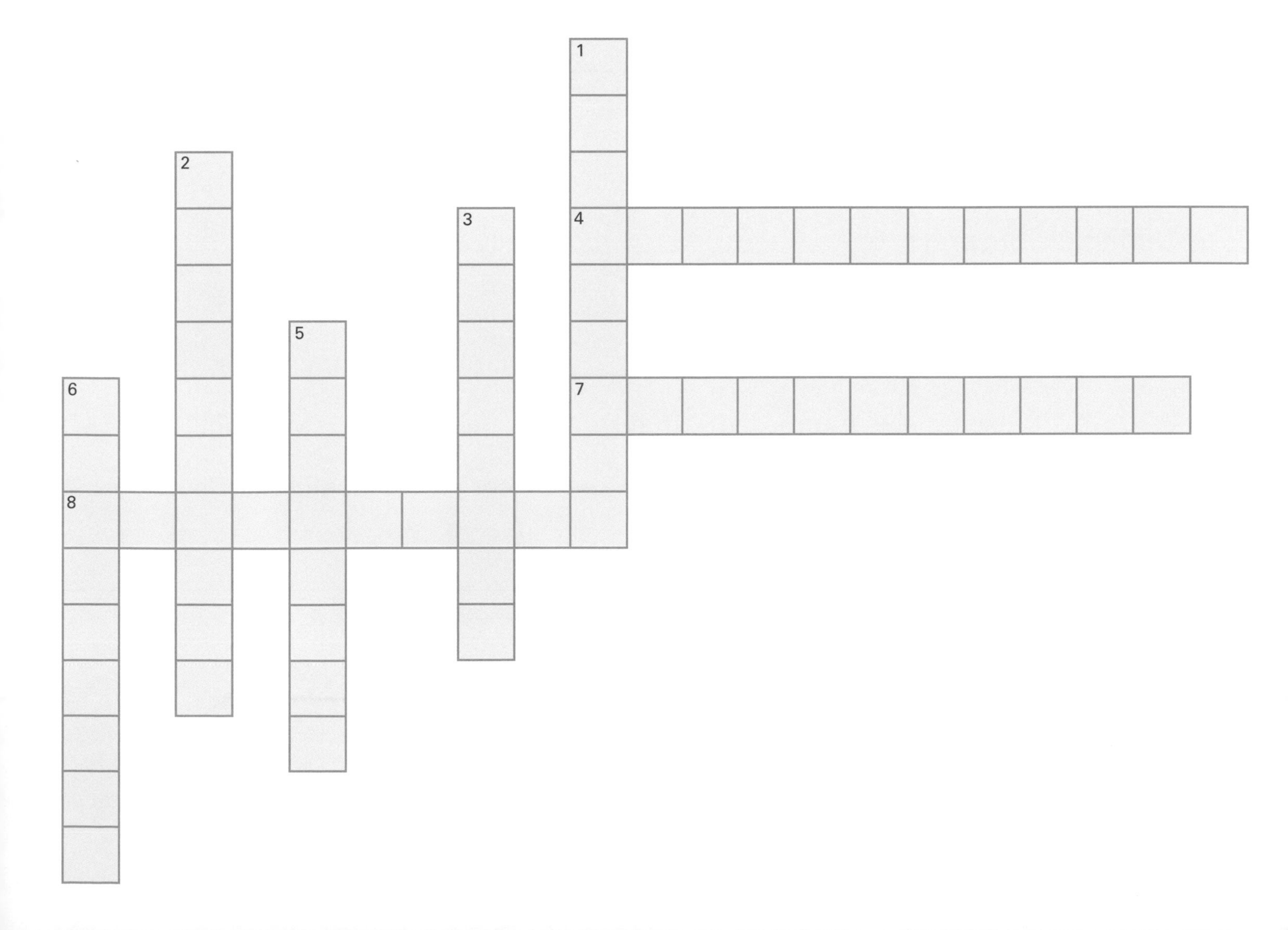

Blank Out!

FILL IN the blanks with keywords.

certainty	construction	creative	education	decisive
explosion	imagination	information	permission	similarity

1. I tried to convince my mom the rock concert would further my musical ________________, but she still wouldn't let me go.
2. When it was time to choose between chocolate cake and apple pie, Lila was ________________.
3. The mall was closed for new ________________.
4. Madeline is like a walking ________________ booth. She knows everything about everyone.
5. During the fireworks, one ________________ really scared my dog.
6. Lucy picked out her outfit with great ________________.
7. Ingrid's mom granted us ________________ to go on the roller coaster.
8. Aaron's art teacher was impressed with his ________________ painting.
9. There is a lot of ________________ between soccer and football, but they are not exactly the same.
10. The science fiction writer had an amazing ________________.

Chopping Block

READ the words. CHOP OFF the suffix in each word by drawing a line right before the ending. WRITE the root word in the blank.

HINT: You may have to add a letter or two to make the root word.

1. combination ____________________
2. invasion ____________________
3. tension ____________________
4. loyalty ____________________
5. migration ____________________
6. option ____________________
7. illustration ____________________
8. invasive ____________________
9. additive ____________________
10. divisive ____________________

Blank Out!

FILL IN the blanks with keywords.

1. You need __________________ to borrow your friend's bike.
2. __________________ is the process of creating a new building, for example.
3. When two chemicals mix, there could be an __________________.
4. Someone who knows exactly what she wants is __________________.
5. Twins usually share more than one __________________.
6. Someone who shows originality and cleverness is __________________.
7. You need to use your __________________ to dream up new ideas.
8. You get __________________ from an encyclopedia.
9. __________________ is knowing something without doubt.
10. __________________ is the result of instruction, training, or study.

Keywords

au•di•ble—AW-duh-buhl *adjective* able to be heard

be•liev•a•ble—bih-LEE-vuh-buhl *adjective* can be considered true

co•lo•ni•al—kuh-LOH-nee-uhl *adjective* referring to the 13 British colonies that became the United States of America

com•fort•a•ble—KUHM-fer-tuh-buhl *adjective* a state of well-being or ease

log•i•cal—LAHJ-ih-kuhl *adjective* resulting from clear thinking

me•tal•lic—mih-TAL-ihk *adjective* made of or containing metal

mu•si•cal—MYOO-zih-kuhl *adjective* having a natural ability to carry a tune or play an instrument

no•tice•a•ble—NOH-tih-suh-buhl *adjective* can be easily observed

po•et•ic—poh-EHT-ihk *adjective* 1. having a rhyming or lyrical quality 2. pleasing to the ear

re•vers•i•ble—rih-VER-suh-buhl *adjective* 1. able to be turned back 2. can be worn inside out

Check It!

Page 66

Read & Replace

1. comfortable
2. audible
3. noticeable
4. metallic
5. musical
6. poetic
7. reversible
8. logical
9. believable
10. colonial

Page 67

Suffix Hopscotch

1. –ic
2. –able
3. -al

Page 68

Match Up

1. official
2. chewable
3. disposable
4. heroic
5. reliable

Page 69

Criss Cross

ACROSS
1. colonial
6. reversible
7. audible
8. logical
9. believable

DOWN
1. comfortable
2. noticeable
3. poetic
4. musical
5. metallic

Read & Replace

READ the story FILL IN the blanks with keywords.

Time Travel

Wendy and her family boarded the plane. She couldn't wait to see her grandparents in Massachusetts. She adjusted her seat to get 1 ________________. The flight attendant's microphone was off, so her speech was not 2 ________________. Wendy put her hand near her ear in a 3 ________________ gesture, and the flight attendant turned on her microphone, and showed how to click the 4 ________________ seat buckle into place.

Wendy hooked her headphone into the armrest. There was one 5 ________________ station with songs from her parents' era. Then there was a station with Shakespeare's sonnets and other 6 ________________ readings. Thankfully, they began to show a movie. It was about a time machine. Since people could go back in time, their mistakes were 7 ________________. There were some 8 ________________ flaws, though, and the whole story was not very 9 ________________.

Wendy was very glad to get off the plane. She gave her grandparents a big hug. "Guess where we're taking you!" they announced. "We're going to Plymouth Rock to show you our 10 ________________ history."

"Great!" thought Wendy. "More travel—back in time again!"

Check It!

Page 70

Blank Out!

1. audible
2. noticeable
3. musical
4. comfortable
5. believable
6. reversible
7. logical
8. colonial
9. poetic
10. metallic

Page 71

Chopping Block

1. mistake
2. sense
3. history
4. melody
5. optic
6. teach
7. robot
8. volcano
9. remove
10. value

Page 72

Blank Out!

1. logical
2. musical
3. colonial
4. audible
5. reversible
6. poetic
7. noticeable
8. metallic
9. comfortable
10. believable

Suffix Hopscotch

LOOK AT the root words in each hopscotch board. FILL IN the matching suffix at the top of the board.

HINT: Sometimes you have to drop or change a letter when you add a suffix.

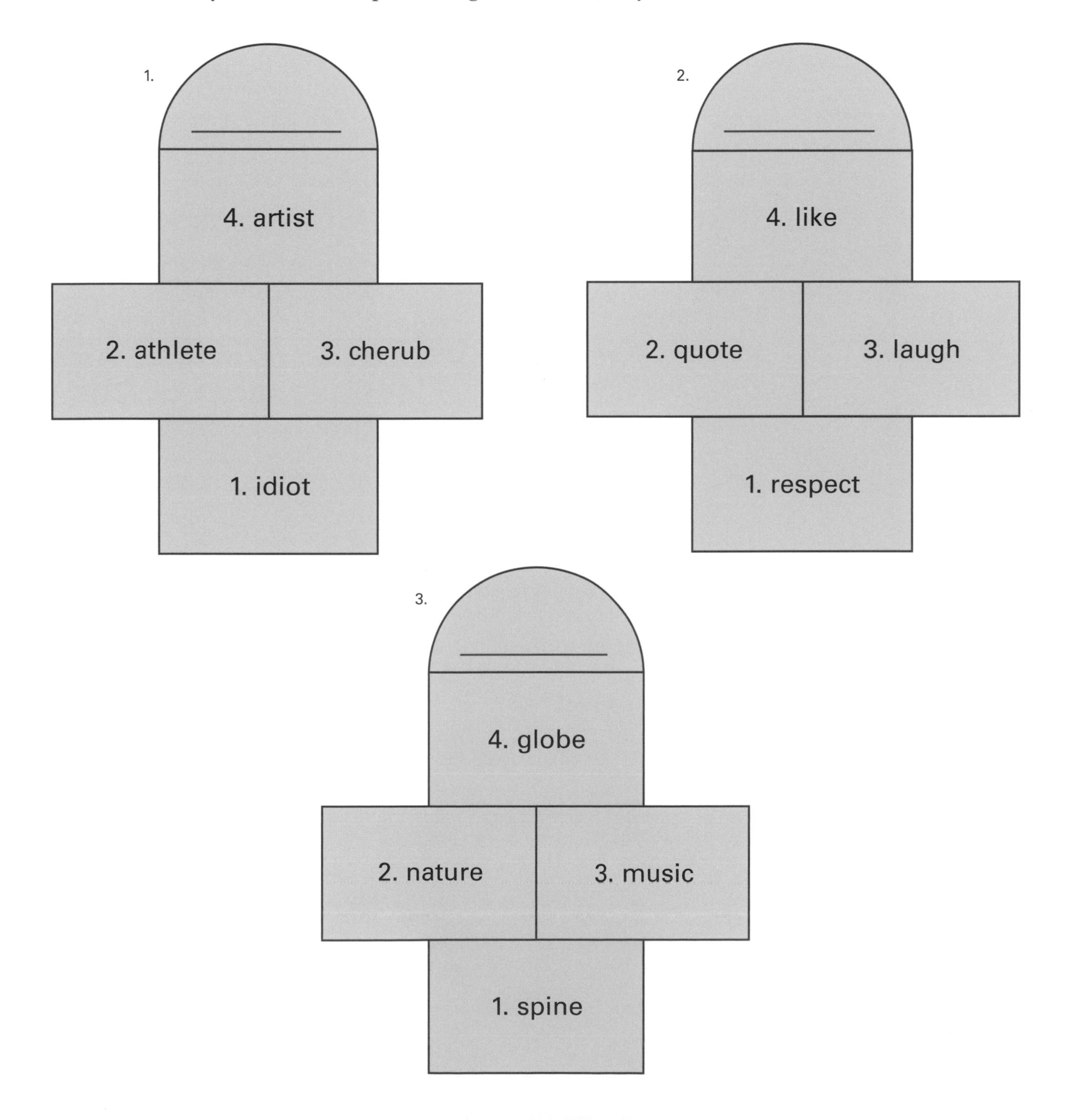

Match Up

MATCH each root to a suffix. Then WRITE the word next to its definition.

Suffix Meanings: *-able, -ible = is able to* *-al, -ial, -ic = relating to*

Root	Suffix
office	-ic
chew	-ial
dispose	-able
hero	-able
rely	-able

	Word	Definition
1.	______________	having formal authority
2.	______________	can use one's teeth to eat
3.	______________	the act of getting rid of something
4.	______________	doing acts of bravery
5.	______________	able to be counted on

Criss Cross

FILL IN the grid by answering the clues with keywords.

ACROSS

1. American period beginning in the 1600s
6. Can be worn inside-out
7. Not silent
8. Making sense
9. Seems possible

DOWN

1. Being relaxed with a pillow and blanket
2. Can be easily seen
3. Having lovely and flowing language
4. A play filled with songs
5. Something made of metal

Blank Out!

FILL IN the blanks with keywords.

1. George played his music so loudly that it was __________________ down the street.
2. Her new haircut was so __________________ that everyone commented on it.
3. I can't carry a tune, but my brother is very __________________.
4. Please make yourself __________________ while you wait for me.
5. The excuse Susie gave her dad after coming home late wasn't very __________________.
6. I like both sides of my __________________ coat.
7. Lily made a very __________________ argument to get her mom to let her go to the party.
8. Ruth's family took a trip to Williamsburg, Virginia to see __________________ life in action.
9. Shakespeare's writing is very __________________.
10. We hung __________________ decorations for the disco party.

Chopping Block

READ the words. CHOP OFF the suffix in each word by drawing a line right before the ending. WRITE the root word in the blank.

HINT: You may have to add a letter or two to make the root word.

1. mistakable ____________________
2. sensible ____________________
3. historic ____________________
4. melodic ____________________
5. optical ____________________
6. teachable ____________________
7. robotic ____________________
8. volcanic ____________________
9. removal ____________________
10. valuable ____________________

Blank Out!

FILL IN the blanks with keywords.

1. An argument that makes sense is _________________.
2. Someone who can play many instruments is _________________.
3. European settlers who came to America in the 1600s had to adjust to _________________ life in their new land.
4. Something that isn't silent is _________________.
5. Something that can be worn inside-out is _________________.
6. Something that rhymes is _________________.
7. Something you can observe is _________________.
8. Magnets will only stick to _________________ surfaces.
9. When you're in a big easy chair by a fire, you feel _________________.
10. A realistic story is _________________.

Prefix Mix & Match

Think you've got your prefixes straight? It's time to check your skills. LOOK AT the prefixes and root words. WRITE all the words you can make by adding the prefixes to the roots.

anti-	im-	inter-	multi-	tri-
bi-	in-	mis-	trans-	uni-

cycle	centennial	biotic	pod
annual	match	national	perfect
continental	exact	focal	verse

Page 73

Prefix Mix & Match

antibiotic
bicycle
biannual
bicentennial
bifocal
bipod
imperfect
inexact
intercontinental
international
inverse
mismatch
multinational
transcontinental
transverse
triannual
tricentennial
tricycle
trifocal
tripod
unicycle
universe

Page 74

Suffix Mix & Match

allergic, arrival, collectible, collection, collective, combinable, combination, completion, correctible, correction, corrective, divisible, division, divisive, erasable, historic, historical, imaginable, imagination, imaginative, locatable, location, lovable, loyalty, magical, mistakable, partial, partition, removable, removal, scenic, spatial, starvation, technicality, washable

Suffix Mix & Match

Now it's time to test your knowledge of suffixes. LOOK AT the suffixes and root words. WRITE all the words you can make by adding the suffixes to the roots.

-able	-ative	-ic	-itive	-sion
-al	-ial	-ion	-ity	-sive
-ation	-ible	-ition	-ive	-ty

allergy	correct	locate	part	technical
arrive	divide	love	remove	wash
collect	erase	loyal	scene	
combine	history	magic	space	
complete	imagine	mistake	starve	

Check It!

Page 75

Pathfinder

selection, mismatch, confusion, transplant, invention

Page 76

Sniglets!

1. antiloner
2. unisocks
3. translunch
4. ingymable
5. trimessaging

Pathfinder

Think you know your prefixes and suffixes pretty well? Then you'll have no problem with this game. Begin at START. When you get to a box with two arrows, pick the prefix or suffix you can add to the root word. Then follow the prefix or suffix to the next root word. If you make all the right choices, you'll end up at FINISH.

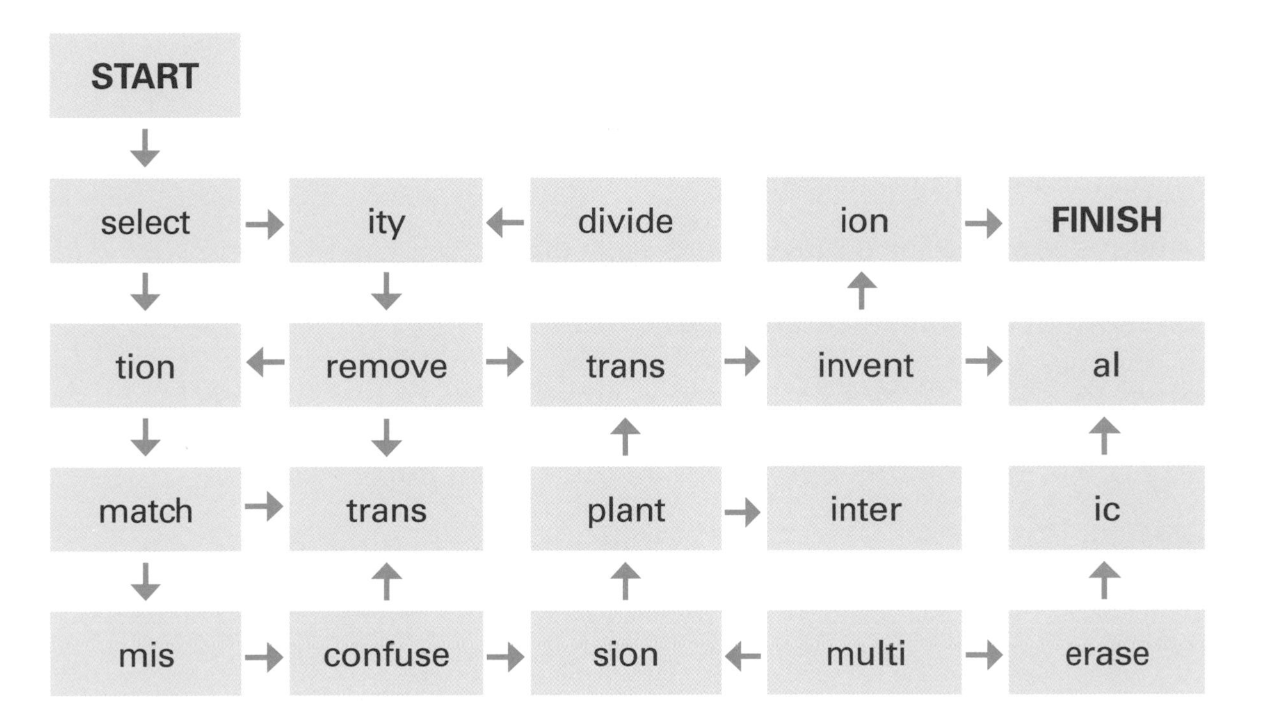

Sniglets!

Are you ready for some more sniglet fun? Remember, sniglets are fun-sounding words that haven't made it to the dictionary yet. Here are some sniglets made with the prefixes and suffixes you just reviewed.

unisocks—single, mismatched socks in your laundry basket
translunch—to swap lunches with a friend
trimessaging—emailing, texting, and IMing at the same time
antiloner—someone who does not like to be alone
ingymable—unable to participate in gym

WRITE a sniglet from the list to complete each sentence.

1. Dave is always looking for a party—he's such an ________________.
2. Kylie wore sandals because all she could find were ________________.
3. Mary hoped to ________________ since she didn't like her sandwich.
4. After Perry broke his toe, his dad wrote a note saying Perry was ________________.
5. Willa was so busy ________________ that she didn't study for her test.

BONUS!

Now it's your turn. Here are some prefixes and suffixes you can use to create more sniglets.

magni- = large	tele- = distant
pro- = favor, for	co- = together

-arium = place for	-holic = addict
-cule = small	-ulent = full of

WRITE DOWN your sniglets and their definitions.

____

____

____

____

____

____

It's a Zoo in Here!

Other cultures have had a big influence on the English language. In fact, many of the animals you'll see at the zoo wouldn't have the names they have now if it weren't for the Greek, Portuguese, Arabic, and other people who named them many, many years ago. MATCH each animal name to its original name.

1. cobra
2. dinosaur
3. giraffe
4. rhinoceros
5. gazelle
6. buffalo
7. flamingo
8. hippopotamus
9. zebra
10. emu

a. zevro
b. boubalos
c. deinos sauros
d. flamengo
e. rhīnōkers
f. ema
g. çobra de capello
h. zirāfa
i. ġazāl
j. hippopotamos

Check It!

Page 77

It's a Zoo in Here!

1. g
2. c
3. h
4. e
5. i
6. b
7. d
8. j
9. a
10. f

Page 78

Let's Eat!

Greek: baklava, spanakopita, gyro, feta, pita
French: crepe, mayonnaise, sauce, quiche
Mexcian: chili, salsa, quesadilla

Page 79

First Words

P	Y	W	I	G	W	A	M	U	M	S	R	H	N	Y
A	E	R	M	H	W	P	A	O	O	B	Q	I	C	B
S	M	R	O	S	I	Z	V	B	C	M	X	U	Q	Y
C	E	Q	S	K	S	T	W	I	C	X	G	K	A	T
L	Z	T	C	I	C	W	D	R	A	A	Y	J	O	W
W	R	V	N	F	M	I	G	A	S	R	X	B	H	T
U	S	X	L	T	L	M	H	C	I	F	O	S	L	E
K	A	Y	A	K	E	Y	O	K	N	G	A	U	Q	P
K	W	A	H	A	M	O	T	N	G	U	K	R	E	E
A	Z	C	W	P	R	D	O	A	Q	H	J	V	M	E
M	Z	X	Y	P	N	B	N	S	E	R	B	Q	H	Z
E	B	S	E	W	F	I	Y	F	J	S	W	Q	T	J
M	J	C	B	K	Z	G	R	F	U	E	V	X	E	W
R	A	D	T	O	I	A	R	I	U	O	P	J	P	Y
N	I	O	W	O	L	Q	S	V	E	B	X	N	U	L

Page 80

Music to Our Ears

1. bongo
2. cello
3. guitar
4. karaoke
5. symphony
6. waltz
7. juke box

Let's Eat!

Already hungry again? Let's grab some more snacks from around the globe. Can you figure out where these foods comes from?

DRAW a line from each food to its plate.

First Words

Now it's time to unpack your bags! There are many English words that didn't travel at all to reach our shores. In fact, they came from the people who had been living here for thousands of years.

SEARCH the letters up, down, and diagonally to find words that came from our Native American past.

hickory moccasin persimmon squash squaw tepee
toboggan wigwam tomahawk caribou pecan kayak

P Y W I G W A M U M S R H N Y

A E R M H W P A O O B Q I C B

S M R O S I Z V B C M X U Q Y

C E Q S K S T W I C X G K A T

L Z T C I C W D R A A Y J O W

W R V N F M I G A S R X B H T

U S X L T L M H C I F O S L E

K A Y A K E Y O K N G A U Q P

K W A H A M O T N G U K R E E

A Z C W P R D O A Q H J V M E

M Z X Y P N B N S E R B Q H Z

E B S E W F I Y F J S W Q T J

M J C B K Z G R F U E V X E W

R A D T O I A R I U O P J P Y

N I O W O L Q S V E B X N U L

Music to Our Ears

Music is sometimes called a language without borders. Everyone can listen and hear the same beautiful sounds. And it's true—people from all countries have banged, whistled, and strummed for thousands of years.

READ about the origins of these musical terms. Then UNSCRAMBLE the answers.

1. This instrument for drumming was named in the Congo.

   gnobo ________________

2. This large Italian instrument is plucked and bowed.

   olecl ________________

3. Named in Spain, this instrument is strummed.

   tauigr ________________

4. People in Japan were the first to sing along to music with this machine.

   okkaare ________________

5. A large group of different instruments were first played together in Greece.

   shonyymp ________________

6. People often dance to this three-beat music in Germany.

   ztwal ________________

7. People first use this device to choose their own songs in West Africa.

   kuej xbo ________________

Keywords

air•port—EHR-port *noun* level area where aircraft can take off and land

hab•it—HAB-iht *noun* something done often, by routine

hab•i•tat—HAB-ih-TAT *noun* an environment for human beings or other living things

ha•bit•u•al—huh-BIHCH-oo-uhl *adjective* done by habit

in•hab•it—ihn-HAB-iht *verb* to live somewhere

por•ta•ble—POR-tuh-buhl *adjective* able to be carried

por•ter—POR-ter *noun* someone who carries baggage

re•port—rih-PORT *noun* a detailed statement, paper, or account about a topic

sup•port—suh-PORT *verb* to hold something or bear weight

trans•port—trans-PORT *verb* to take from one place to another

Check It!

Page 82

Read & Replace

1. porter
2. portable
3. habit
4. habitual
5. transport
6. airport
7. report
8. inhabit
9. support
10. habitat

Page 83

Root It Out!

1. porter
2. support
3. habit
4. inhabit
5. habitat
6. transport
7. habitual
8. portable
9. report
10. airport

Page 84

Stack Up

HAB
1. rehabilitate
2. cohabit
3. uninhabited
4. haberdashery

PORT
1. import
2. important
3. export
4. deport

Page 85

Criss Cross

ACROSS
4. habitat
7. portable
8. support
10. transport

DOWN
1. habit
2. habitual
3. inhabit
5 airport
6. report
9. porter

Read & Replace

ROOTS are groups of letters that can be found at the beginning, middle, or end of a word. Each root has its own meaning:

The root *hab* in the middle of the word *inhabit* means *hold* or *live*.
The root *port* at the end of the word *transport* means *carry*.

READ the story. FILL IN the blanks with keywords.

Their vacation was over. Mia's family had their bags packed. Her mother's suitcase was so big the 1 ________________ had to carry it to the lobby. "Do you have a 2 ________________ washing machine in there?" her father teased. Their mom had a 3 ________________ of overpacking, and her dad was a 4 ________________ jokester. A van came to 5 ________________ them to the 6 ________________. Mia noticed dark clouds in the sky. Her brother, Jack, launched into his annoying newscaster voice "Special 7 ________________. Hurricane warning. Expect travel to be disrupted." Mia rolled her eyes.

When the family arrived at the terminal, the building was packed. Flights were being cancelled. "It's getting serious, folks. Passengers may have to 8 ________________ the building." Jack announced. Many were sleeping on their luggage.

Mia sat down on the floor and leaned against a column for 9 ________________. "It's going to be a long evening," she sighed. "I guess I'll study the 10 ________________ of Gate 36!"

Check It!

Page 86

Blank Out!

1. portable
2. habit
3. airport
4. habitat
5. habitual
6. transport
7. report
8. inhabit
9. support
10. porter

Page 87

It's Puzzling!

cohabit
important
rehabilitate

Page 88

Blank Out!

1. transport
2. support
3. airport
4. habitat
5. habitual
6. report
7. habit
8. porter
9. inhabit
10. portable

Root It Out!

READ each definition. WRITE the missing root letters in the blanks.

hab = have, hold, or live   *port = carry*

HINT: The **bold words** give you a clue about the root.

1. someone who **carries** your bags ___ ___ ___ ___ er
2. **carry** weight sup___ ___ ___ ___
3. a pattern of behavior that you **have** ___ ___ ___ it
4. to **live** in a place in___ ___ ___it
5. the environment where someone **lives** ___ ___ ___itat
6. to **carry** something from one place to another trans___ ___ ___ ___
7. **having** a repeated pattern of activity ___ ___ ___itual
8. can be **carried** ___ ___ ___ ___able
9. a paper that **carries** lots of information re___ ___ ___ ___
10. a place with planes that **carry** people to faraway places air___ ___ ___ ___

Stack Up

FILL IN a root in each word. WRITE the word in the column with that root. LOOK UP the definition. Can you see how it's related to its root?

re__________ilitate

im__________

co__________it

im__________ant

ex__________

de__________

unin__________ited

__________erdashery

HAB | PORT

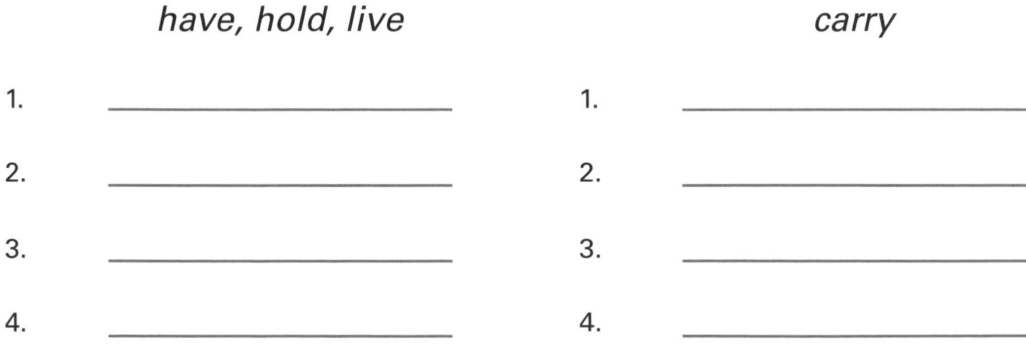

Criss Cross

FILL IN the grid by answering the clues with keywords.

ACROSS

4. To help animals thrive, we must protect their ___.
7. You can take a laptop with you because it is ___.
8. Something to lean on
10. The subway can ___ passengers.

DOWN

1. Picking your nose is a bad ___.
2. Something you frequently do is ___.
3. Aliens might do this to Mars
5. Leave plenty of time to check in here
6. A kind of card with letter grades on it
9. Someone who will get your bags

Blank Out!

FILL IN the blanks with keywords.

1. Lenny brought a ________________ stove on the camping trip.
2. Zoey had a gross ________________ of chewing her nails and spitting them out the window on car trips.
3. When they left town, the Coopers took a taxi to the ________________.
4. Max says his brother belongs in a rainforest ________________ with other monkeys.
5. My neighbor drives me crazy with his ________________ 6 a.m. leaf-blowing and lawn mowing!
6. My sister had to use a wagon to ________________ all her stuffed animals to the park.
7. After the concert, Nellie gave a glowing ________________ to her friend about the new band.
8. My little brother's like a space alien—weird ideas ________________ his brain.
9. Henry's grandmother uses a cane for extra ________________.
10. The ________________ asked Tom if he had rocks in his suitcase, they were so heavy!

It's Puzzling!

MATCH a prefix, root, and suffix to form a word. WRITE the words in the blanks.

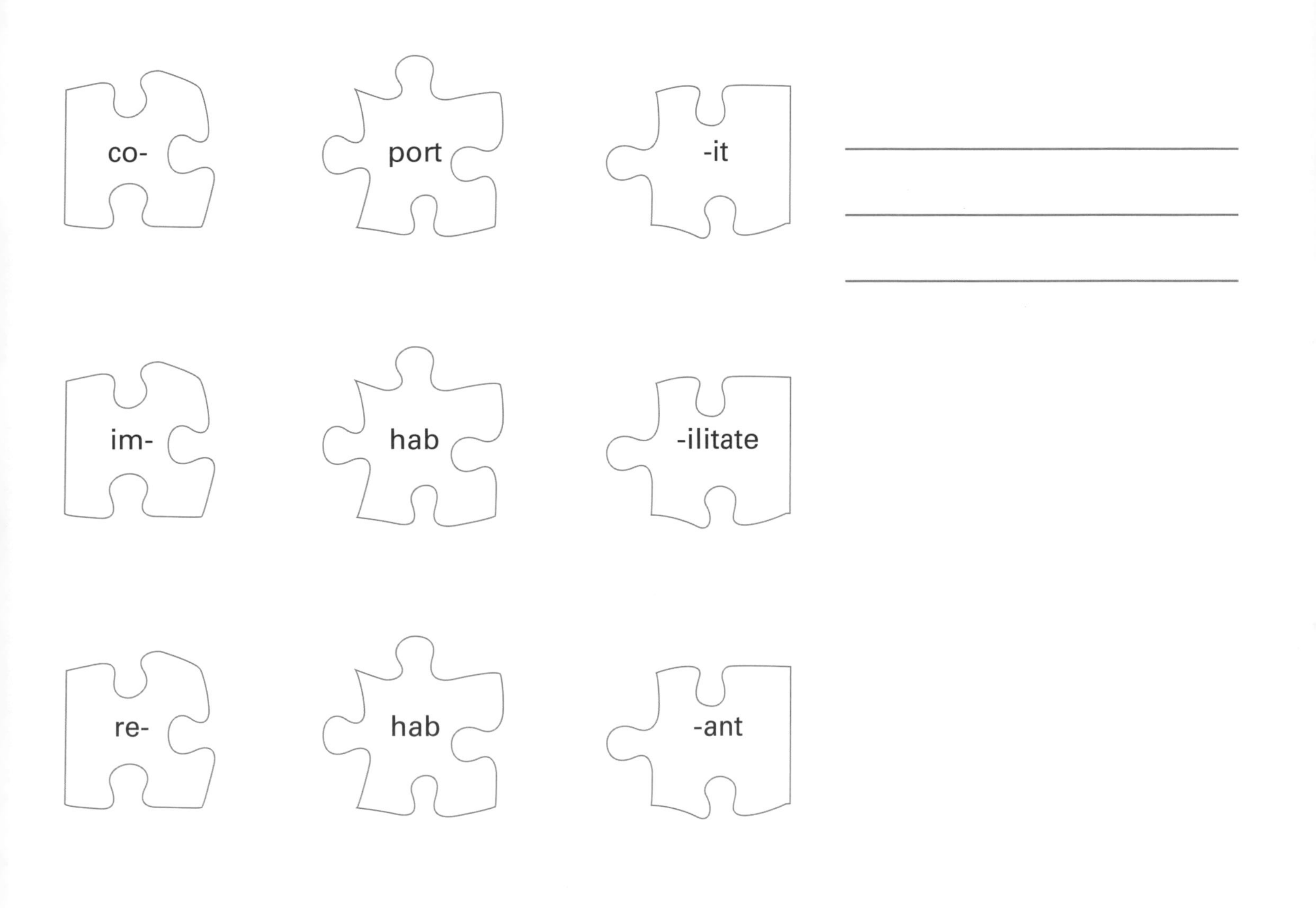

Blank Out!

FILL IN the blanks with keywords.

1. This word tells how you get something to another place.

   You ________________ it.

2. My sister turned to me for this when she argued with our parents to stay up late.

   ____

3. This word tells where you might go to pick up a visitor. ________________
4. This word is what a hollowed out tree might be, for an owl. ________________
5. Jay wears the same grubby grey sneakers every day because he's this kind of

   person. ________________

6. This word tells what you might file with the police if your bike was stolen.

   ____

7. Cracking your knuckles is one example of this. ________________
8. I felt like I had this job when Mom made me carry in all the groceries.

   ____

9. When you leave food on the counter, a colony of ants might do this to your kitchen.

   They might ________________ it.

10. An inflatable mattress, a 10-inch TV, and a folding table all have this in common. They are all ________________.

Keywords

ad•ver•tise—AD-ver-tiz *verb* to promote a product or service

at•tract—uh-TRAKT *verb* to pull something towards something else

con•trac•tion—kuhn-TRAK-shuhn *noun* the process of becoming smaller

con•vert•i•ble—kuhn-VER-tuh-buhl *adjective* able to change in form

dis•tract—dih-STRAKT *verb* to draw attention away from something

sub•tract—suhb-TRAKT *verb* to take away

trac•tion—TRAK-shuhn *noun* pulling power

trac•tor—TRAK-ter *noun* a large farm vehicle used to pull equipment

ver•ti•cal—VER-tih-kuhl *adjective* straight up and down

ver•ti•go—VER-tih-goh *noun* dizzying sensation of whirling motion

Check It!

Page 90

Read & Replace

1. attract
2. convertible
3. subtract
4. advertise
5. tractor
6. traction
7. vertigo
8. distract
9. contraction

Page 91

Root It Out!

1. contraction
2. vertical
3. attract
4. convertible
5. advertise
6. distract
7. vertigo
8. tractor
9. subtract
10. traction

Page 92

Stack Up

VERT
1. invert
2. vertebra
3. extrovert
4. introvert

TRACT
1. retractable
2. protract
3. extract
4. detract

Page 93

Criss Cross

ACROSS
1. vertical
5. attract
8. vertigo
9. subtract

DOWN
2. contraction
3. traction
4. convertible
6. advertise
7. distract

Check It!

Page 94

Blank Out!

1. convertible
2. traction
3. advertise
4. distract
5. vertigo
6. attract
7. subtract
8. tractor
9. contraction
10. vertical

Page 95

It's Puzzling!

diverted
extracted
extraction
extractable
introverted
reverted
retracted
retractable

Page 96

Blank Out!

1. vertigo
2. advertise
3. distract
4. vertical
5. attract
6. traction
7. contraction
8. convertible
9. tractor
10. subtract

Read & Replace

The root *vert* at the beginning of the word *vertical* means *turn*, as in something turned on its end. The root *tract* at the end of the word *attract* means *pull*, as in two things pulled towards each other. Read the story. FILL IN the blanks with keywords.

advertise	attract	contraction	convertible	distract
subtract	traction	tractor	vertical	vertigo

Rosa and Samantha were waiting to order at the diner. Rosa picked up an ad for cars. "Which ones do you like?" she asked.

"The sporty ones 1 ______________ me. I like this cool red 2 ______________ car," said Samantha. "If I could only 3 ______________ a few thousand dollars from the price!"

"Hey, I guess farmers 4 ______________ in here," Rosa laughed. "Check out this giant 5 ______________. It might work great in the snow, with all that 6 ______________," she added.

"I don't know," said Samantha. "I think I'd get 7 ______________ climbing up that high." Just then the waitress came up. "I don't mean to 8 ______________ you, young ladies," she said. "But are you ready to order?"

"I'll have the 'VertiBurger'" said Rosa.

"What's that?" asked Samantha.

"It's our tallest burger," answered the waitress. "VertiBurger's a 9 ______________ for Vertical Burger," she explained.

"Better not try one," said Rosa, "or you'll get dizzy!"

Root It Out!

READ each sentence. WRITE the missing root letters in the blanks.

vert = turn *tract = pull*

1. When you drop some letters and **pull** two words together, you form a con___ ___ ___ ___ ___ion.
2. When you **turn** something flat on its end, you make it ___ ___ ___ ___ical.
3. Bright lights always at___ ___ ___ ___ ___ tons of bugs.
4. You can **turn** a con___ ___ ___ ___ible sofa into a bed.
5. A new product can **turn** into a big hit if you ad___ ___ ___ ___ise it.
6. Having the television on can **pull** your attention away and dis___ ___ ___ ___ ___ you from your book.
7. If the room seems to **turn** around and you feel dizzy, you may have ___ ___ ___ ___igo.
8. When a farmer needs to **pull** heavy farm equipment, he hitches it to his ___ ___ ___ ___ ___ or.
9. If you **pull** some money out of the bank, don't forget to sub___ ___ ___ ___ ___ it from your balance.
10. We tried to **pull** the sled up the hill but it was so slippery that it was hard to get ___ ___ ___ ___ ___ ion.

Stack Up

FILL IN a root in each word. WRITE the word in the column with that root.

LOOK UP the definition. Can you see how it's related to its root?

vert = turn   tract = pull

in______________

re______________able

pro______________

______________ebra

extro______________

intro______________

ex______________

de______________

VERT/VERS	TRACT
turn	*pull*
1. ______________	1. ______________
2. ______________	2. ______________
3. ______________	3. ______________
4. ______________	4. ______________

Criss Cross

FILL IN the grid by answering the clues with keywords.

ACROSS

1. Not horizontal
5. What magnets sometimes do to another
8. Head spinning feeling
9. Take away

DOWN

2. "Don't" instead of "do not"
3. What you get when you get a grip
4. Vehicle with a retracting roof
6. Promote
7. Take your mind off something

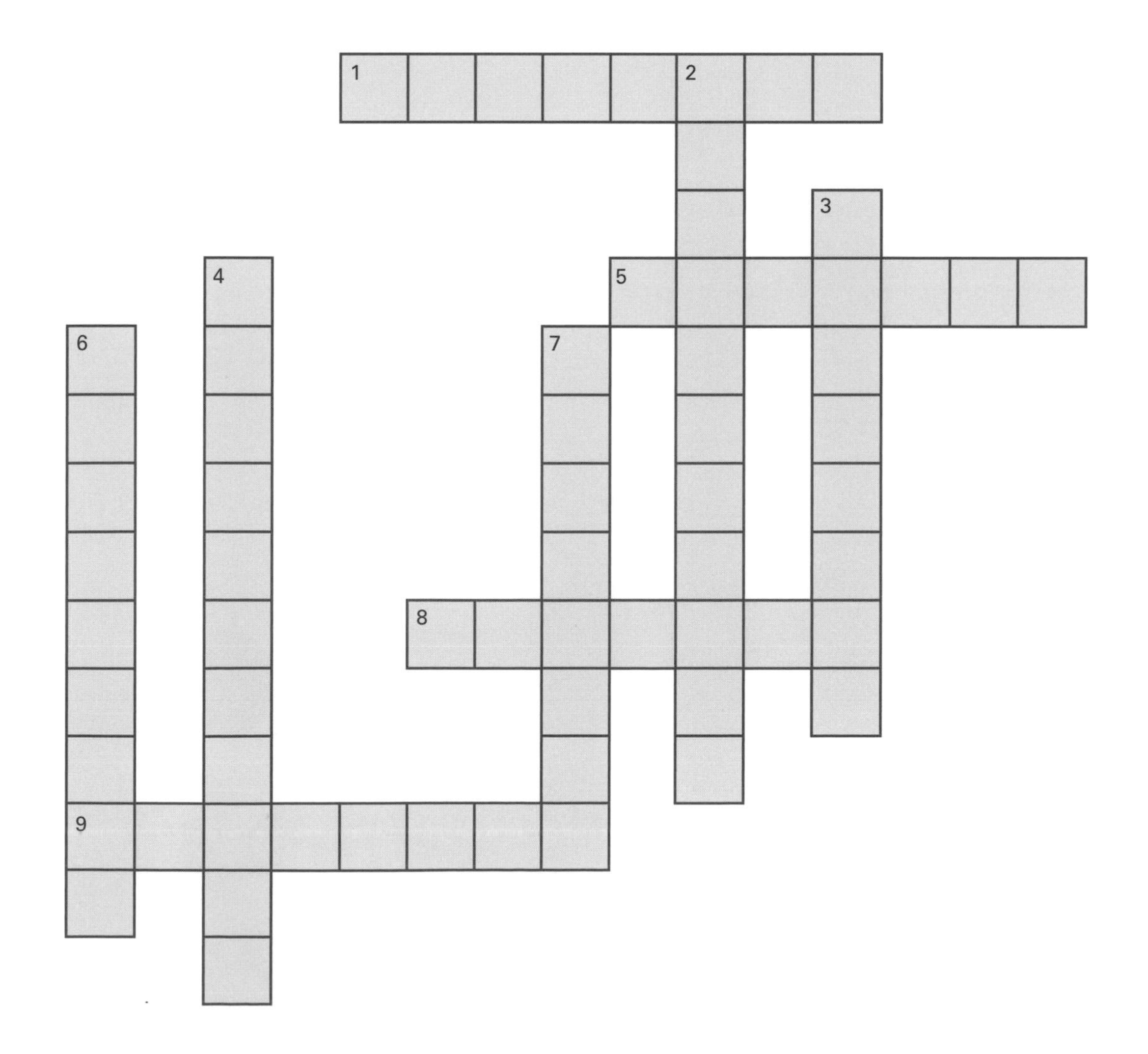

Blank Out!

FILL IN the blanks with keywords.

advertise	attract	contraction	convertible	distract
subtract	traction	tractor	vertical	vertigo

1. Sasha's toy was a _________________ bulldozer that could turn into an army tank.
2. Ryan needed soccer cleats to get better _________________ on the field.
3. If you want to get pet-sitting jobs, _________________ in the local paper.
4. The cheerleaders tried to _________________ the other team with their shouts and boos.
5. At the state fair, the ferris wheel gave Aunt Lin _________________.
6. Jen thought her perfume would _________________ boys, but it really smelled like dirty socks!
7. With this coupon, you can _________________ $10 from your total purchase.
8. We hitched up the boat to a _________________ to pull it to the lake.
9. Brad used a _________________ to keep his text message as short as possible.
10. When I startled my cat, she did a crazy _________________ leap.

It's Puzzling!

MATCH a prefix, root, and suffix to form a word. WRITE the words in the blanks.

HINT: You can use the same prefix, root, and suffix more than once.

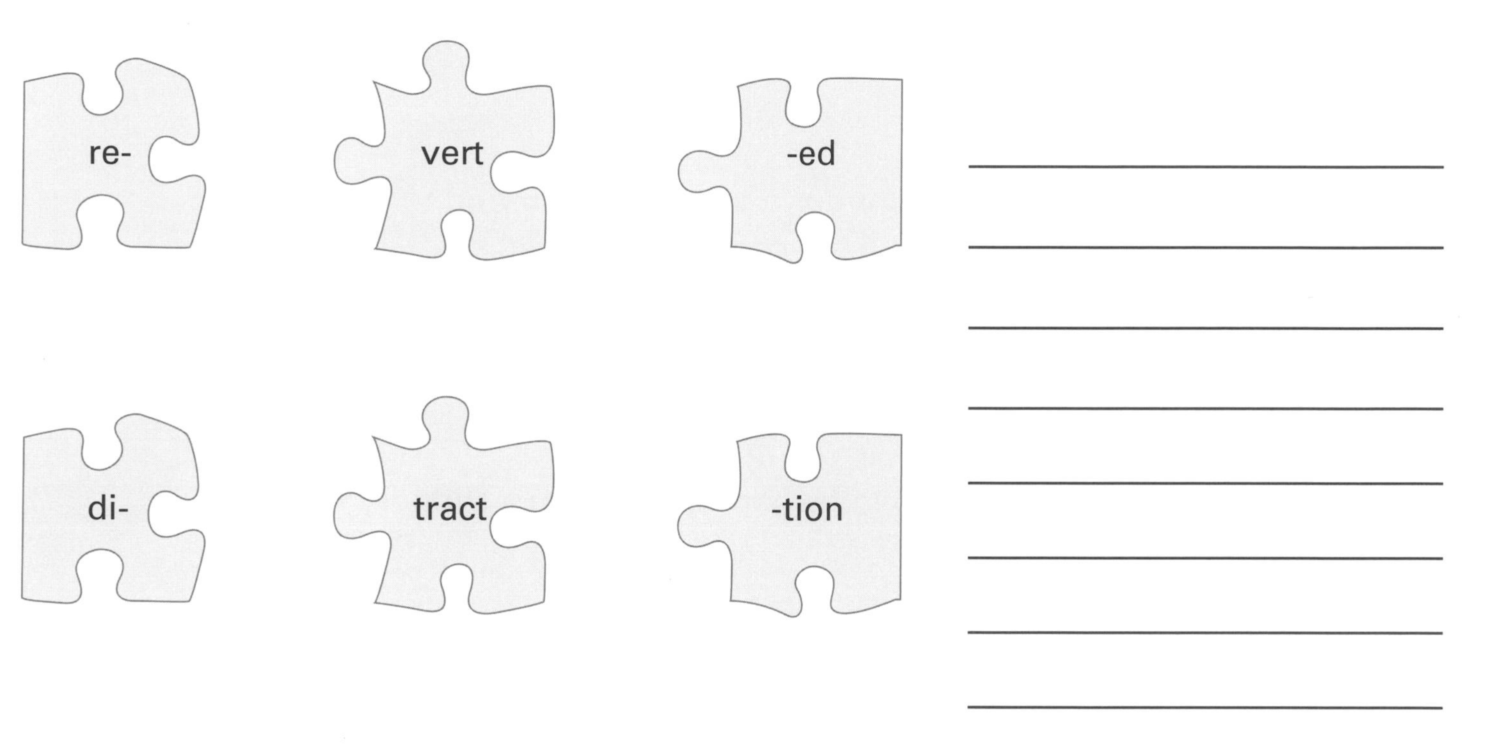

Blank Out!

FILL IN the blanks with keywords.

1. "Jerry is so tall. I'm surprised he doesn't get ________________."
2. Barry's such a gossip. He likes to ________________ my personal info to everyone we know.
3. This word tells what noise might do to you if you're trying to concentrate. ________________
4. This word describes your position when you're standing up. ________________
5. You might plant special bushes to do this to butterflies. ________________
6. This word tells what you try to get when climbing up a slippery slope. ________________
7. If you join two words together and drop a letter or two, you make this. ________________
8. My sister thinks my bedroom is ________________ and jumps and slides all over everything as if it was a playground too.
9. At the state fair, I saw people actually having this kind of race with their farm equipment. ________________
10. This word tells what you need to do to turn 10 into 7. ________________

Keywords

de•hy•drat•ed—dee-HI-dray-tuhd *verb* having the water removed from

hy•drant—HI-druhnt *noun* a discharge pipe for drawing water from a main pipe

hy•drate—HI-drayt *verb* to cause to absorb water

hy•dro•gen—HI-druh-jihn *adjective* a colorless gas that combines with oxygen to form water

hy•dro•pho•bi•a—HI-druh-FOH-bee-uh *noun* fear of water

ther•mal—THER-muhl *adjective* of or relating to heat

ther•mom•e•ter—ther-MAHM-ih-ter *noun* a device used for taking temperature

ther•mos—THER-muhs *noun* a container that keeps beverages hot or cold

ther•mo•stat—THER-muh-stat *noun* a device that regulates temperature

Check It!

Page 98

Read & Replace

1. hydrant
2. Thermal
3. thermos
4. hydrate
5. thermometer
6. dehydrated
7. thermostat
8. hydrogen
9. hydrophobia

Page 99

Root It Out

1. dehydrated
2. hydrant
3. thermal
4. thermometer
5. thermostat
6. hydrophobia
7. hydrogen
8. thermos
9. hydrate

Page 100

Combo Mambo

THERM

1. thermonuclear
2. thermodynamics
3. thermoelectric

HYDR

1. hydroplane
2. hydraulic
3. hydroelectric

Page 101

Criss Cross

ACROSS

2. thermal
6. hydrogen
8. hydrant
9. thermostat

DOWN

1. thermos
3. hydrate
4. hydrophobia
5. thermometer
7. dehydrated

Read & Replace

Here are some more roots to add to your collection. The root *hydr* in the word *hydrate* means *water*. The root *therm* in the word *thermometer* means *heat*. READ the story. FILL IN the blanks with keywords.

Our camping trip was almost a disaster. It started out smoothly enough. We met at the fire 1 ________________ near the corner to wait for the bus. Hallie, the leader, asked us to check our backpacks. She called out a list. 2 ________________ underwear? Check! Flashlight? Check! 3 ________________ bottle? Check! Hallie reminded us it's important to 4 ________________ ourselves on our hikes. "The 5 ________________ showed the temperature was off the charts today," she warned. "It's going to be a scorcher."

We took a long hike up a steep hill. We were all huffing and puffing with our packs on our backs. Suddenly I noticed my friend Liz didn't look good... and then she fainted. It turns out she was 6 ________________. Hallie told us her body's 7 ________________ had overheated. Thankfully she recovered when we gave her some H_2O (that's two molecules of 8 ________________ + oxygen = water!)

After that, we were glad to get to the campsite. Everyone was eager to take a swim in the lake. Except Anna, that is. She was shaking like a leaf. It turns out she has 9 ________________ and was afraid to get anywhere near the lake!

Check It!

Page 102

Blank Out!

1. hydrate
2. hydrophobia
3. dehydrated
4. thermal
5. thermos
6. hydrant
7. thermostat
8. hydrogen
9. thermometer

Page 103

It's Puzzling!

dehydrate
dehydration
geothermal
rehydrate
rehydration

Page 104

Blank Out!

1. hydrant
2. dehydrated
3. thermostat
4. hydrophobia
5. thermal
6. hydrate
7. thermos
8. thermometer
9. hydrogen

Root It Out

READ the sentences. WRITE the missing root letters in the blanks to complete each keyword.

1. When you lose too much **water** you get de___ ___ ___ ___ated.
2. When a firefighter needs to hook his hose up to a **water** source, he looks for a ___ ___ ___ ___ant.
3. If you decide to go sledding, you'll want to stay conserve your **heat** with ___ ___ ___ ___ ___al leggings.
4. When you want to measure the **heat** outside, you look at the ___ ___ ___ ___ ___ometer.
5. When it gets really cold, you turn the **heat** up on the ___ ___ ___ ___ ___ostat.
6. If a person is really scared of **water**, he has ___ ___ ___ ___ophobia.
7. One of the two elements that combine to make **water** is ___ ___ ___ ___ogen.
8. If you don't want your soup to lose **heat**, you can put it in a ___ ___ ___ ___ ___ os.
9. To help your seeds grow, ___ ___ ___ ___ate them.

Combo Mambo

MATCH a word ending in a blue box to a root in a green box to make a word. WRITE the word in the root word box. LOOK UP the definition. Can you see how the word is related to *heat* or *water*?

HINT: You can use a word ending more than once.

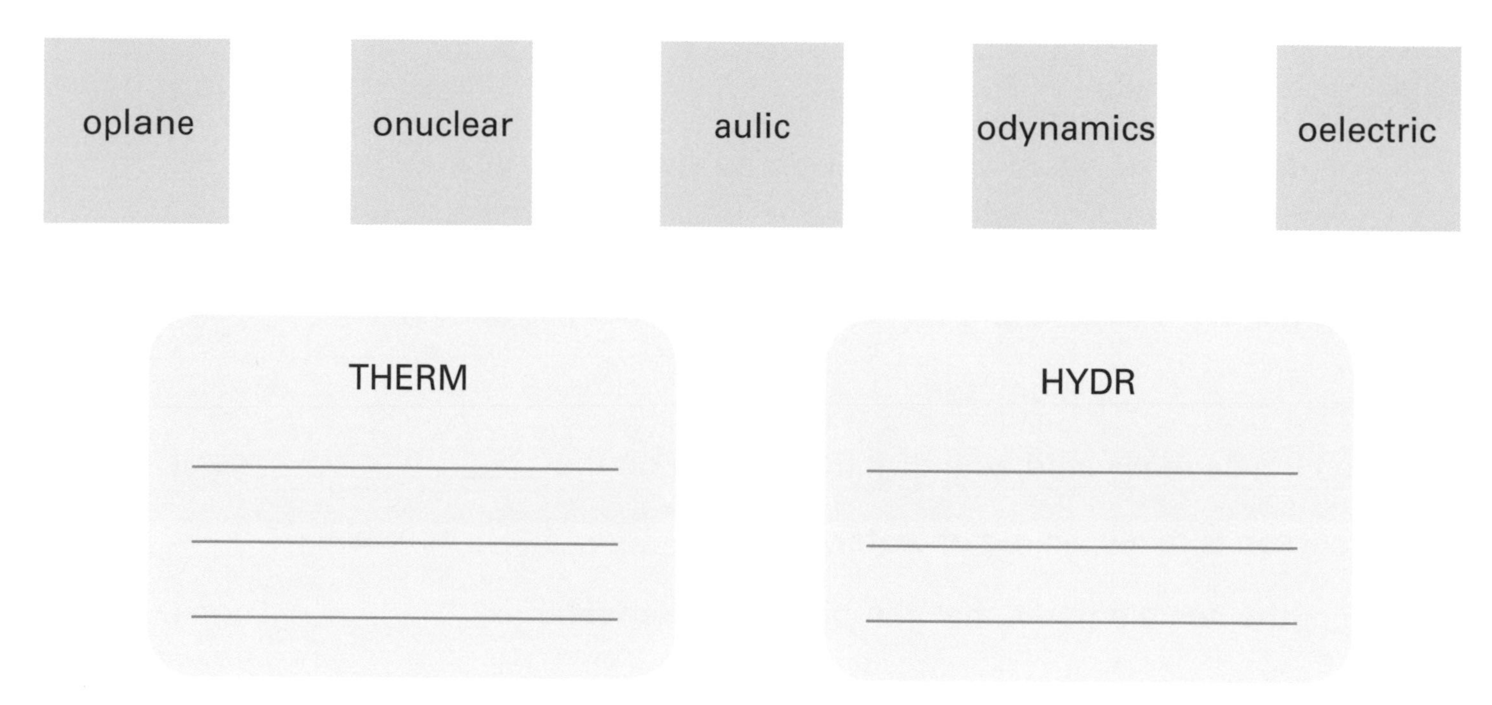

Criss Cross

FILL IN the grid by answering the clues with keywords.

ACROSS

2. This kind of blanket can keep you warm
6. The "H" in H_2O
8. Don't park near a fire ______.
9. Turn this down to save energy in the winter

DOWN

1. Something to keep hot cocoa warm
3. Give liquid to
4. Fear of water
5. Tool used to check your temperature
7. Dried up

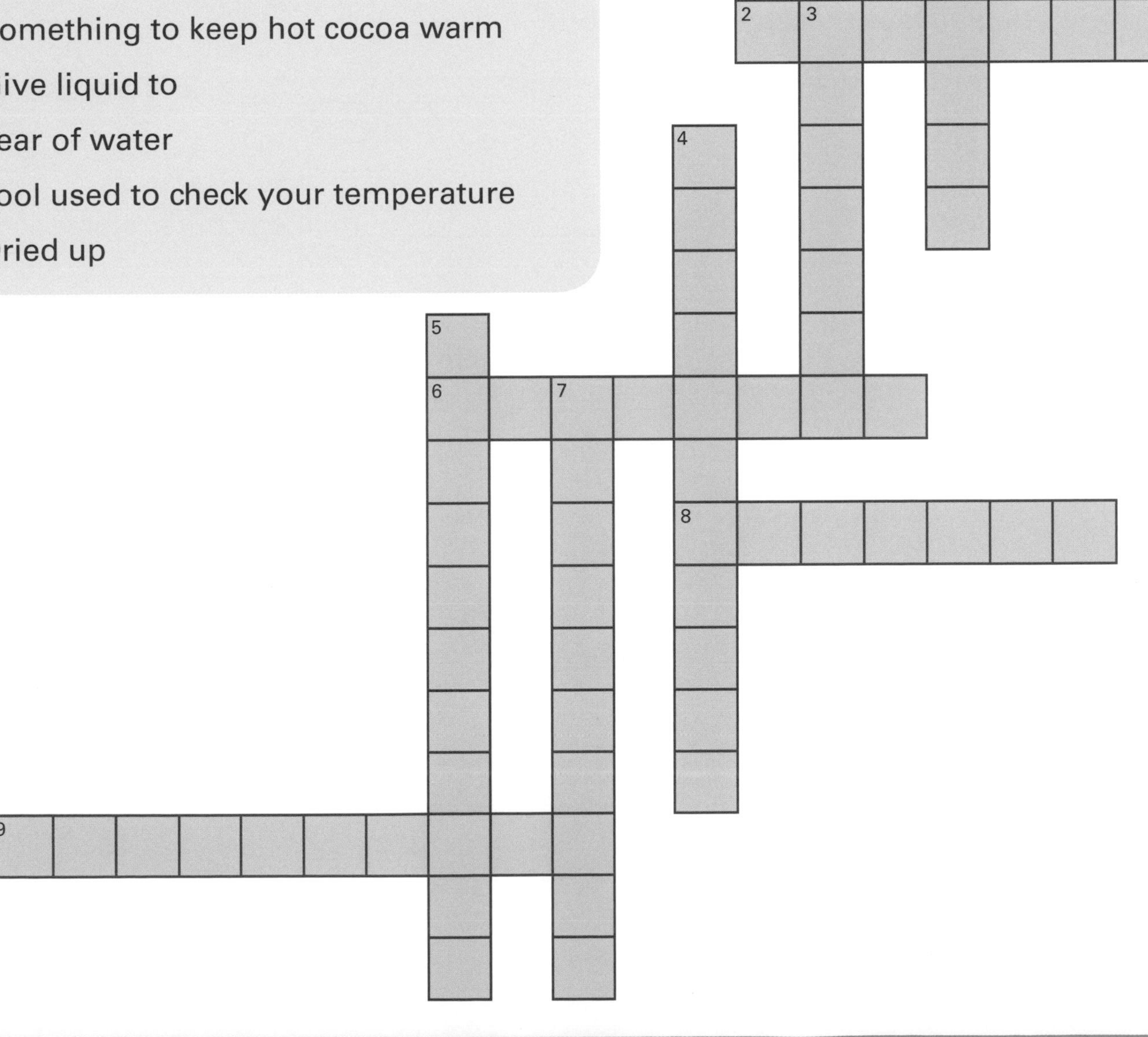

Blank Out!

FILL IN the blanks with keywords.

1. Drink a lot of water to ________________ yourself during the tennis match.
2. Paul overcame his ________________ by taking swimming lessons.
3. The plants looked a little ________________ when we got back from our trip.
4. Jake's new ________________ gloves kept his hands warm during the snowball fight.
5. Mandy brought cold lemonade in a ________________ to the picnic.
6. Toby's dog always makes a beeline for that fire ________________.
7. My mom turns up the temperature on the ________________, and my dad keeps turning it down!
8. Did you know that there's more ________________ than any other element in the universe?
9. Our oven ________________ broke, and the brownies burned so much that the smoke alarm went off.

It's Puzzling!

MATCH a prefix, root, and suffix to form a new word. WRITE the words in the blanks.

HINT: You can use the same prefix, root, and suffix more than once.

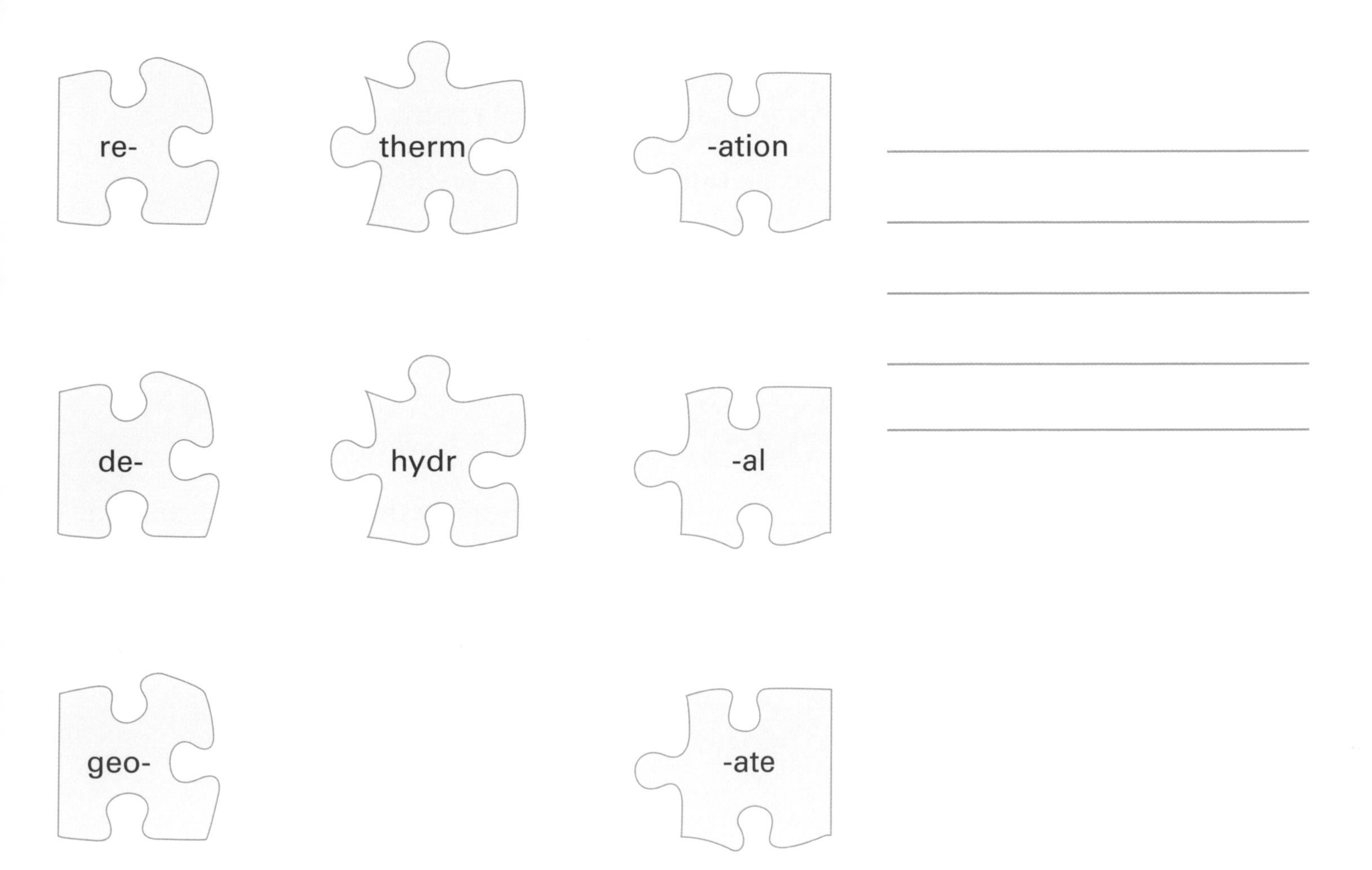

Blank Out!

FILL IN the blanks with keywords.

1. A __________________ has a water pipe coming out of the street.
2. Someone who's very, very thirsty is __________________.
3. You use a __________________ to turn up the heat in a room.
4. Peter has __________________, so he refused to go the water park with us.
5. __________________ underwear keeps you warm.
6. We handed out cups of water at the marathon to help __________________ the runners.
7. You should put hot tea in a __________________ to keep it warm.
8. Caleb watched the __________________ like a hawk, hoping the rain would change to snow.
8. When __________________ combines with oxygen, you get water.

Keywords

ad•e•quate—AD-ih-kwiht *adjective* enough to satisfy

con•duct—KAHN-duhkt *noun* the way a person acts

de•duc•tion—dih-DUK-shuhn *noun* the act of subtracting something

e•qual•i•ty—ih-KWAL-ih-tee *noun* the state of being the same as

e•qua•tion—ih-KWAY-zhuhn *noun* a mathematical statement in which two sides are equal

e•qua•tor—ih-KWAY-ter *noun* an imaginary line drawn around the middle of the earth

e•qui•dis•tant—EE-kwih-DIHS-tuhnt *adjective* equally distant

eq•ui•ta•ble—EHK-wih-tuh-buhl *adjective* even-handed or fair

in•tro•duce—ihn-truh-DOOS *verb* to make someone known to another person

pro•duce—pruh-DOOS *verb* to make something

Check It!

Page 106

Read & Replace

1. introduce
2. produce
3. equator
4. equidistant
5. equation
6. adequate
7. deduction
8. equitable
9. conduct
10. equality

Page 107

Root It Out

1. equidistant
2. introduce
3. conduct
4. adequate
5. produce
6. equation
7. deduction
8. equator
9. equality
10. equitable

Page 108

Stack Up

EQU
1. equilibrium
2. equinox
3. equilateral

DUC/DUCT
1. aqueduct
2. reproduce
3. viaduct

Page 109

Criss Cross

ACROSS
2. equation
3. produce
7. equidistant
8. deduction

DOWN
1. introduce
2. equality
4. adequate
5. equator
6. conduct

Read & Replace

The root *equ* in the word *equal* means *the same*. The root *duct* in the word *conduct* means *lead*. Read the story. FILL IN the blanks with keywords.

Yesterday, my family went to the planetarium. We saw a new 3-D movie about our galaxy. First, the museum director came out to 1 ________________ the film. He was very proud because he helped 2 ________________ it.

Then, the lights went out and suddenly stars and planets were swirling around us. "You are standing on the middle of Planet Earth, right on the 3 ________________," boomed a deep voice. "You are 4 ________________ from the North and South poles." For a moment, I felt lost in the galaxy. But then the booming voice started rattling off a long 5 ________________ about how to calculate the distance of different planets. I thought I was back in math class! Just the sight of the stars would have been 6 ________________ without all of the explanations.

"Will there be a quiz at the end?" I whispered to my sister.

"Yes, and you'll get an automatic 7 ________________ of 20 points for talking during the movie," she whispered back. "Then so will you," I pointed out, to be 8 ________________.

My parents shushed us. "You guys have terrible 9 ________________. If you want 10 ________________," my dad said, "you can *both* go wait in the car!"

Check It!

Page 110

Blank Out!

1. deduction
2. equitable
3. conduct
4. introduce
5. equality
6. equator
7. adequate
8. equidistant
9. produce
10. equation

Page 111

It's Puzzling!

conductive
induction
inequity
reproduction
reproductive
unequivocal

Page 112

Blank Out!

1. equator
2. deduction
3. equidistant
4. adequate
5. Equality
6. produce
7. equitable
8. conduct
9. introduce
10. equation

Root It Out

READ each sentence. WRITE the missing root letters in the blanks.

duc, duct = lead   equ, equi, equa = even, just

1. If two things are an **equal** distance apart from something they are ___ ___ ___ ___distant.
2. I **led** my friend to meet my mother so that I could intro___ ___ ___e them.
3. When you **lead** by example you demonstrate good con___ ___ ___ ___.
4. If something is just okay but could be better, it is ad___ ___ ___ ___te.
5. The baseball coach tried to **lead** the team to pro___ ___ ___e more hits.
6. The numbers on both sides of the equals sign are **even** in an ___ ___ ___ ___tion.
7. "The clues **lead** me to one elementary de___ ___ ___ ___ion," said Sherlock Holmes.
8. The ___ ___ ___ ___tor is an **even** distance from Earth's two poles.
9. People must receive **even**-handed treatment for true ___ ___ ___ ___lity.
10. The pieces of cake were so **uneven** that it's not ___ ___ ___ ___table that my brother got the bigger piece!

Stack Up

FILL IN a root in each word. WRITE the word in the column with that root. LOOK UP the definition. Can you see how it's related to its root?

duc, duct = lead   *equ, equi, equa = even, just*

_______________librium

aque_______________

_______________nox

repro_______________

_______________lateral

via_______________

EQU /EQUI/ EQUA	DUC/DUCT
same	*lead*
1. ____________	1. ____________
2. ____________	2. ____________
3. ____________	3. ____________

Criss Cross

FILL IN the grid by answering the clues with keywords.

ACROSS

2. 52 + 6 = 58
3. Make
7. Two objects equally far from a place
8. Something taken away

DOWN

1. Help two people meet each other
2. Fairness
4. Just enough
5. An invisible line around the middle of the globe
6. Behavior

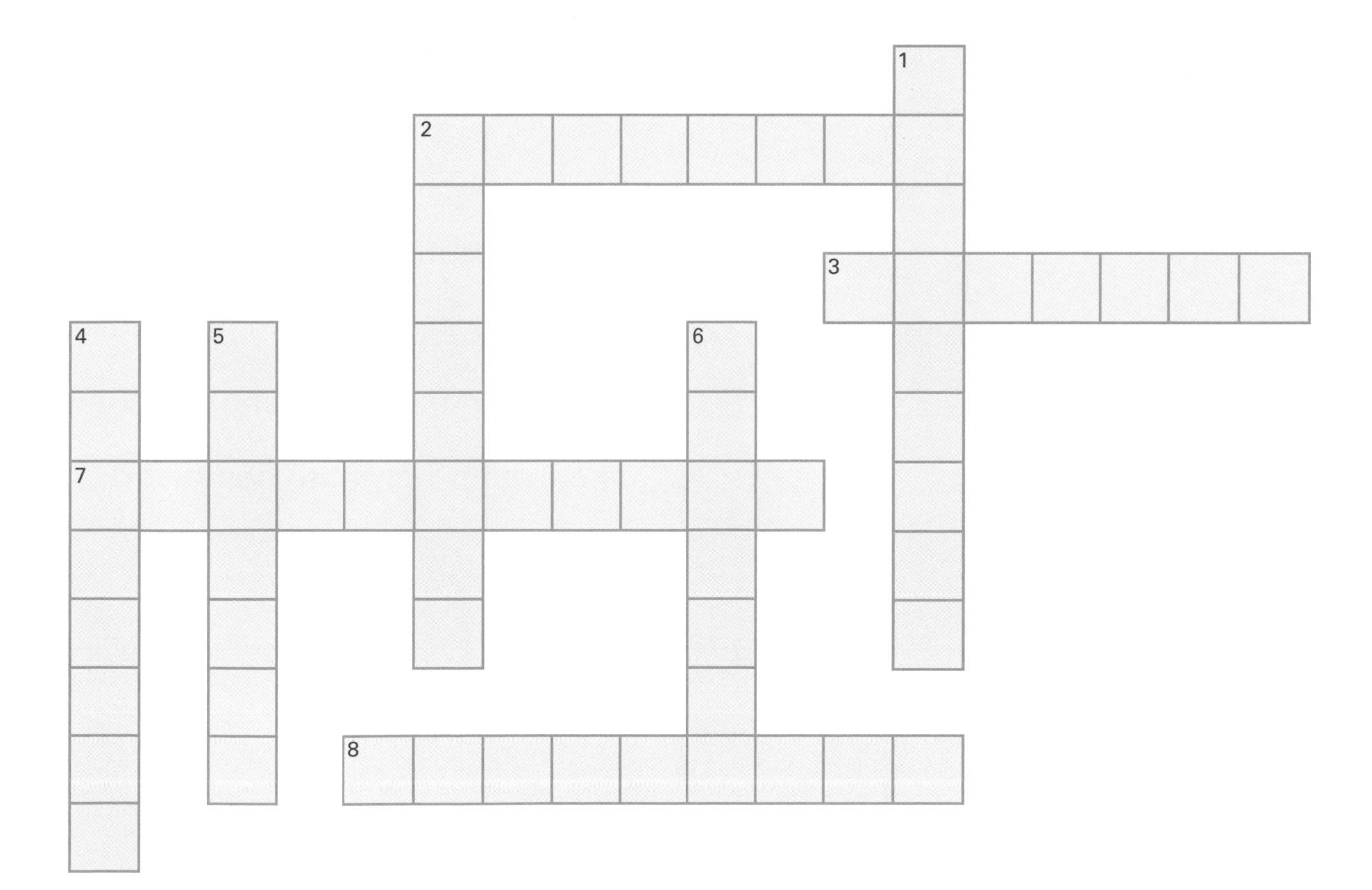

Blank Out!

FILL IN the blanks with keywords.

1. My parents paid for the game but said they'd make a ________________ from my allowance.
2. After the job, the babysitters divided the payment in an ________________ manner.
3. The police gave the hero who stopped the robber a medal for brave ________________.
4. Lila worked up her nerve to ________________ herself to the new boy on the block.
5. Civil rights leaders marched for ________________ for all people.
6. The Earth is hottest near the ________________.
7. Make sure to leave ________________ room for dessert.
8. We tried to pick a meeting place that was ________________ from our houses.
9. Maya's band hopes to ________________ a CD when they have enough songs.
10. Lindsay had one more ________________ to solve for her math homework.

It's Puzzling!

MATCH a prefix, root, and suffix to form a word. WRITE the words on the blanks.

HINT: You can use the same prefix, root, and suffix more than once.

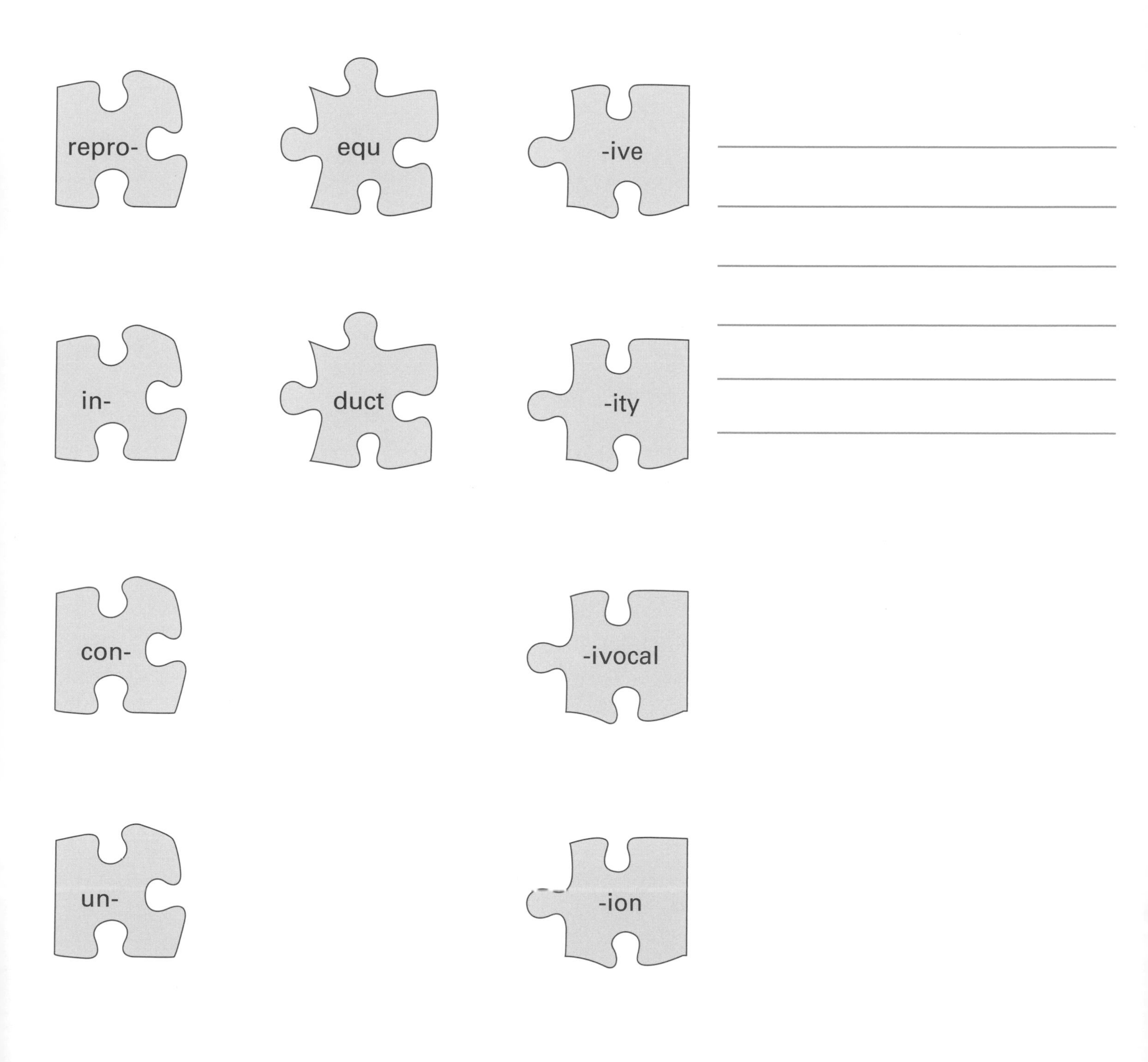

Blank Out!

FILL IN the blanks with keywords.

1. If you dislike hot weather, you would not want to live near the _________________.
2. A _________________ is a conclusion drawn from several observations.
3. The legs on my hemmed pants are not _________________ from the floor. I look lopsided!
4. Something that's just good enough is _________________.
5. _________________ is when all people have the same rights.
6. Factory machines can _________________ games quickly.
7. An even-handed solution is an _________________ one.
8. Members of our Troop are bound by a code of good _________________.
9. You might _________________ to two friends who don't know each other at your birthday party
10. This word names a mathematical statement that contains an equals sign.
____

Pick the One!

You know your roots, right? So get going and check your skills! LOOK AT each group of words. Then CIRCLE the real word in each row.

Hint: Check to see if the words you find are in a dictionary!

1.	inhydrible	inhabitant	portity
2.	univert	supportive	habify
3.	tritractation	transvertate	rehabilitate
4.	thermoport	conducive	rehydrophobe
5.	irreversible	equatity	antiduct
6.	mishabitate	importitude	introduction
7.	heliport	hydratical	revertical
8.	inthermia	equilibrium	transhabible
9.	retraction	misduce	multitherm
10.	intractial	misport	hydraulic

BONUS!

Pick a word from the list that is not a real word. Use what you know about prefixes, suffixes, and roots to write a definition. Use the "word" in a sentence.

____

____

____

____

Check It!

Page 113

Pick the One!

1. inhabitant
2. supportive
3. rehabilitate
4. conducive
5. irreversible
6. introduction
7. heliport
8. equilibrium
9. retraction
10. hydraulic

Page 114

Match Up

Answers and suggested words:
1. c; hydrate, dehydrated, hydrogen
2. f; equation, equator, equality
3. h; habit, inhabit, habitual
4. g; thermal, thermos, thermometer
5. a; report, transport, portable
6. d; tractor, traction, distract
7. b; conduct, deduction, introduce
8. e; vertical, vertigo, advertise

Page 115

Pathfinder

import, introvert, distract, inhabit, extract

Page 116

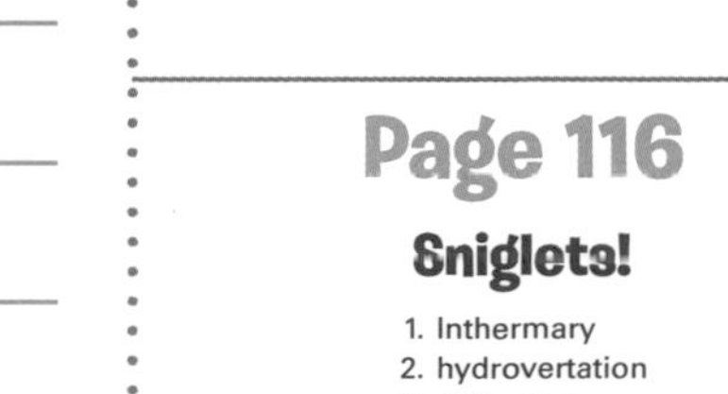

Sniglets!

1. Inthermary
2. hydrovertation
3. ridicuport
4. habitipal
5. dustraction

Match Up

MATCH each root to its meaning. Then WRITE three words that contain each root.

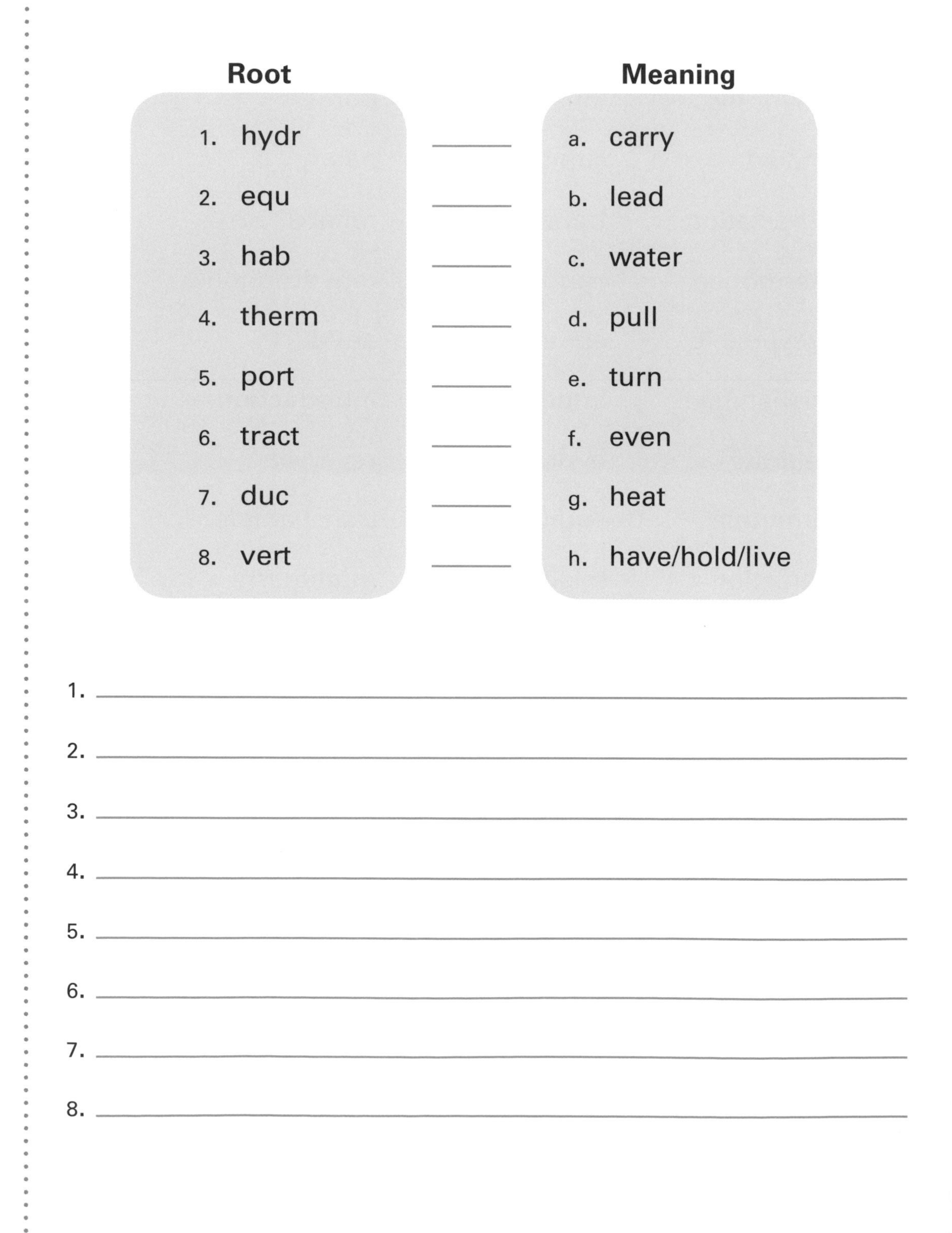

Root		Meaning
1. hydr	____	a. carry
2. equ	____	b. lead
3. hab	____	c. water
4. therm	____	d. pull
5. port	____	e. turn
6. tract	____	f. even
7. duc	____	g. heat
8. vert	____	h. have/hold/live

1. ______________________________
2. ______________________________
3. ______________________________
4. ______________________________
5. ______________________________
6. ______________________________
7. ______________________________
8. ______________________________

Pathfinder

The game's the same, only the roots change. Begin at START. When you get to a box with two arrows, pick the root that you can add to the prefix. Then follow the prefix or suffix to the next root word. If you make all the right choices, you'll end up at FINISH.

START		hydra		tract	→	in	→	habit
↓		↓		↑		↓		↓
im	→	port		dis	→	therm	←	ex
↓		↓		↑		↑		↓
therm		intro	→	vert	←	port		tract
↓		↓				↑		↓
hydra		tract	→	therm	←	hab		**FINISH**

Sniglets!

Here are some sniglets made with the roots you just reviewed.

ridicuport—having far too much stuff to carry
hydrovertation—the ability to do somersaults in the water
inthermary—a place where overheated people go to cool off
dustraction—dust balls and lint that cling like glue to surfaces
habitipal—someone with whom you share a habit

WRITE a sniglet from the list to complete each sentence.

1. On scorching hot summer days, we call Josh's pool "The ________________."
2. This summer, Milo planned to practice his ________________ at the pool.
3. Kerry's backpack had so many books it was ________________.
4. When it came to shooting spitballs at lunch, Dave was my ________________.
5. After sleeping under the couch, our cat Fluffy was a walking lint ball, covered with ________________!

Now it's your turn. Here are some roots you can use to create more sniglets. Use what you know about prefixes, suffixes, and roots to write a definition for each. The sillier the better!

cap = head (as in captain)
rupt = break (as in rupture)
mit = sent (as in transmit)
val = strong (as in value)
reg = rule (as in regulation)

____

____

____

____

____

Index

ad•dress[1]—uh-DREHS *verb* 1. to speak about an issue 2. to deal with

ad•dress[2]—A-drehs *noun* information that gives the location of someone's home or business or e-mail account

ad•e•quate—AD-ih-kwiht *adjective* enough to satisfy

ad•ver•tise—AD-ver-tiz *verb* to promote a product or service

air•port—EHR-port *noun* level area where aircraft can take off and land

al•lowed—uh-LOWD *verb (past tense)* permitted

a•loud—uh-LOWD *adverb* 1. using the voice 2. not silently

a•muse—uh-MYOOZ *verb* 1. to charm or entertain 2. to make smile or laugh. Synonyms: charm, entertain, delight. Antonyms: bore, tire.

an•ti•bac•te•ri•al—AN-tee-bak-TEER-ee-uhl *adjective* active in killing germs

an•ti•slav•er•y—AN-tee-SLAY-vuh-ree *adjective* against the practice of owning people

an•ti•so•cial—AN-tee-SOH-shuhl *adjective* not wanting to be with other people

at•tract—uh-TRAKT *verb* to pull something towards something else

au•di•ble—AW-duh-buhl *adjective* able to be heard

be•liev•a•ble—bih-LEE-vuh-buhl *adjective* can be considered true

bi•an•nu •al—bi-AN-yoo-uhl *adjective* occurring twice a year

bi•cy•cle—BI-sihk-uhl *noun* a two-wheeled vehicle

bin•oc•u•lars—buh-NOK-yuh-lerz *noun* a magnifying device with two lenses for seeing faraway objects

bud•dy—BUH-dee *noun* friend. Synonyms: pal, friend, chum. Antonyms: enemy, foe.

cer•tain•ty—SER-tuhn-tee *noun* the state of being sure

co•lo•ni•al—kuh-LOH-nee-uhl *adjective* referring to the 13 British colonies that became the United States of America

com•fort•a•ble—KUHM-fer-tuh-buhl *adjective* a state of well-being or ease

con•duct—KAHN-duhkt *noun* the way a person acts

con•struc•tion—kuhn-STRUHK-shuhn *noun* the process of building

con•trac•tion—kuhn-TRAK-shuhn *noun* the process of becoming smaller

con•vert•i•ble—kuhn-VER-tuh-buhl *adjective* able to change in form

creak—kreek *verb* to make a squeaking sound

cre•a•tive—kree-AY-tihv *adjective* capable of making or imagining new things

creek—kreek *noun* a small stream

de•ci•sive—dih-SI-sihv *adjective* having the power to make firm decisions

de•duc•tion—dih-DUK-shuhn *noun* the act of subtracting something

de•hy•drat•ed—dee-HI-dray-tuhd *verb* having the water removed from

dis•con•tin•ue—DIS-kuhn-TIHN-yoo *verb* to stop doing something. Synonyms: stop, end, terminate. Antonyms: continue, proceed, persist.

dis•tract—dih-STRAKT *verb* to draw attention away from something

ed•u•ca•tion—EH-juh-KAY-shuhn *noun* the act of learning or teaching

en•a•ble—ehn-AY-buhl *verb* to make possible. Synonyms: allow, permit, let. Antonyms: prevent, stop, prohibit.

e•qual•i•ty—ih-KWAL-ih-tee *noun* the state of being the same as

e•qua•tion—ih-KWAY-zhuhn *noun* a mathematical statement in which two sides are equal

e•qua•tor—ih-KWAY-ter *noun* an imaginary line drawn around the middle of the earth

e•qui•dis•tant—EE-kwih-DIHS-tuhnt *adjective* equally distant

Index

eq•ui•ta•ble—EHK-wih-tuh-buhl *adjective* even-handed or fair

ex•cuse[1]—ihk-SKYOOS *noun* an explanation given to obtain forgiveness

ex•cuse[2]—ihk-SKYOOZ *verb* to overlook or forgive

ex•plo•sion—ihk-SPLOH-shuhn *noun* a sudden burst, often loud or violent

hab•it—HAB-iht *noun* something done often, by routine

hab•i•tat—HAB-ih-TAT *noun* an environment for human beings or other living things

ha•bit•u•al—huh-BIHCH-oo-uhl *adjective* done by habit

hour—owr *noun* 1. a unit of time equaling 60 minutes 2. the time of day

hy•drant—HI-druhnt *noun* a discharge pipe for drawing water from a main pipe

hy•drate—HI-drayt *verb* to cause to absorb water

hy•dro•gen—HI-druh-jihn *adjective* a colorless gas that combines with oxygen to form water

hy•dro•pho•bi•a—HI-druh-FOH-bee-uh *noun* fear of water

i•mag•i•na•tion—ih-MAJ-uh-NAY-shuhn *noun* the ability of the mind to create

im•mense—ih-MEHNS *adjective* very large. Synonyms: huge, vast, massive. Antonyms: tiny, minute, small.

im•po•lite—IHM-puh-LIT *adjective* 1. rude 2. lacking good manners

im•pos•si•ble—ihm-PAHS-uh-buhl *adjective* not able to occur

in•com•plete—ihn-kuhm-PLEET *adjective* not having all the necessary parts

in•cor•rect—ihn-kuh-REHKT *adjective* not having the right information

in•for•ma•tion—IHN-fer-MAY-shuhn *noun* facts or knowledge gained from any source

in•hab•it—ihn-HAB-iht verb to live somewhere

in•tel•li•gent—ihn-TEHL-uh-juhnt *adjective* smart. Synonyms: smart, bright, clever. Antonyms: stupid, ignorant, dense.

in•ter•na•tion•al—IHN-ter-NASH-uh-nuhl *adjective* between two or more countries

in•ter•sect—IHN-ter-SEHKT *verb* 1. to divide something by going across it 2. to cross or overlap

in•ter•state—IHN-ter-STAYT *adjective* between two or more states

in•tro•duce—ihn-truh-DOOS verb to make someone known to another person

log•i•cal—LAHJ-ih-kuhl *adjective* resulting from clear thinking

me•tal•lic—mih-TAL-ihk *adjective* made of or containing metal

mis•be•have—MIHS-bih-HAYV *verb* to fail to act properly

mis•treat—mihs-TREET *verb* to deal with someone unfairly or cruelly

mis•un•der•stand—MIHS-uhn-der-STAND *verb* to fail to interpret something correctly

mul•ti•col•ored—MUHL-tih-KUHL-erd *adjective* having many hues

mul•ti•cul•tur•al—MUHL-tee-KUHL-cher-uhl *adjective* reflecting many different customs and backgrounds

mul•ti•mil•lion•aire—MUHL-tee-MIHL-yuh-NEHR *noun* someone a person who has millions of dollars

mul•ti•pur•pose—MUHL-tee-PER-puhs *adjective* having more than one use

mu•si•cal—MYOO-zih-kuhl *adjective* having a natural ability to carry a tune or play an instrument

no•tice•a•ble—NOH-tih-suh-buhl *adjective* can be easily observed

our—owr *pronoun* belonging to us

per•mis•sion—per-MIH-shuhn *noun* the act of allowing

plunge—pluhnj *verb* 1. to move abruptly forward or downward 2. to thrust into. Synonyms: dive, plummet. Antonyms: leap, climb.

po•et•ic—poh-EHT-ihk *adjective* 1. having a rhyming or lyrical quality 2. pleasing to the ear

Index

po•lite—puh-LIT *adjective* showing good manners. Synonyms: respectful, courteous. Antonyms: rude, impolite, offensive.

por•ta•ble—POR-tuh-buhl *adjective* able to be carried

por•ter—POR-ter *noun* someone who carries baggage

prin•ci•pal—PRIHN-suh-puhl *noun* 1. the head of a school 2. the main leader of an activitiy or group

prin•ci•ple—PRIHN-suh-puhl *noun* a belief or value that helps guide behavior

prob•a•bly—PRAHB-uh-blee *adverb* very likely. Synonyms: likely, doubtless. Antonyms: unlikely, doubtfully.

pro•duce—pruh-DOOS *verb* to make something

proj•ect[1]—PRAH-jehkt *noun* a task

proj•ect[2]—pruh-JEHKT *verb* 1. to forecast 2. to jut out 3. to say loudly

re•cord[1]—REHK-erd *noun* 1. something official that preserves knowledge or history 2. best performance or greatest achievement

re•cord[2]—ri-KORD *verb* to make an audio, video, or written account of something

re•lax—rih-LAKS *verb* 1. to loosen up 2. to make less strict. Synonyms: unwind, loosen up, calm down. Antonyms: tense up, stiffen, strain.

re•port—rih-PORT *noun* a detailed statement, paper, or account about a topic

re•vers•i•ble—rih-VER-suh-buhl *adjective* 1. able to be turned back 2. can be worn inside out

sighs—siz *verb* breathes out audibly *noun* the sounds of sighing

sim•i•lar•i•ty—SIHM-uh-LAR-ih-tee *noun* the state of having a lot in common

size—siz *noun* 1. how big something is 2. the physical dimensions of an object

sub•tract—suhb-TRAKT *verb* to take away

sup•port—suh-PORT *verb* to hold something or bear weight

ther•mal—THER-muhl *adjective* of or relating to heat

ther•mom•e•ter—ther-MAHM-ih-ter *noun* a device used for taking temperature

ther•mos—THER-muhs *noun* a container that keeps beverages hot or cold

ther•mo•stat—THER-muh-stat *noun* a device that regulates temperature

trac•tion—TRAK-shuhn *noun* pulling power

trac•tor—TRAK-ter *noun* a large farm vehicle used to pull equipment

trans•con•ti•nen•tal—TRANS-kahn-tuh-NEHN-tuhl *adjective* crossing a continent

trans•late—TRANS-layt *verb* to convert one language to another

trans•port—trans-PORT *verb* to take from one place to another

tri•an•gle—TRI-ang-guhl *noun* a shape with three sides

tri•ath•lon—tri-ATH-luhn *noun* a sports event with three different activities

trip•lets—TRIHP-lihts *noun* three children born at the same birth

tri•pod—TRI-pahd *noun* a three-legged stand

u•ni•corn—YOO-nih-korn *noun* an imaginary horse-like animal with a single horn

u•ni•cy•cle—YOO-nih-SI-kuhl *noun* a one-wheeled vehicle

u•ni•verse—YOO-nuh-vers *noun* all planets, space, and matter and energy in one whole

ver•ti•cal—VER-tih-kuhl *adjective* straight up and down

ver•ti•go—VER-tih-goh *noun* dizzying sensation of whirling motion

wound[1]—woond *noun* an injury

wound[2]—wownd *verb* 1. wrapped around something 2. changed direction